JOSHUA
LEADER UNDER FIRE

DONALD K. CAMPBELL

While this book is designed for the reader's personal enjoyment and profit, it is also intended for group study. A Leader's Guide with Victor Multiuse Transparency Masters is available from your local bookstore or from the publisher.

VICTOR BOOKS™
A DIVISION OF SCRIPTURE PRESS PUBLICATIONS INC.
USA CANADA ENGLAND

Unless otherwise noted, Scripture quotations are from the *New American Standard Bible* (NASB), © 1960, 1962, 1968, 1971, 1972, 1973 by The Lockman Foundation, La Habra, California. Other quotations are from the King James Version (KJV) and the *New International Version* (NIV), © 1978 by the New York International Bible Society. Used by permission.

Recommended Dewey Decimal Classification: 222.2
Suggested Subject Headings: BIBLE, OLD TESTAMENT—HISTORY; GEOGRAPHY; BIBLICAL CHARACTERS

Library of Congress Catalog Card Number: 80-60868
ISBN: 0-89693-502-7

CONTENTS

**Dedicated
with deep affection and appreciation
to our children
Steve & Bobbi
Tim
Mary & Mike
Jon**

PREFACE

In America and around the world the search is on for effective leaders. Young people by the hundreds train for Christian leadership but desperately need models to inspire and guide them. The Bible is a rich source and provides many examples of dynamic leadership. Joshua stands out among them as a man who was vigorous, forthright, and fearless.

But Joshua did not face an easy task. The Canaanites were fierce people. Their cities were fortified, their armies were kept in fighting condition, and their land was primarily mountainous, making invasion and conquest difficult.

Joshua would need a strong faith in God. He would also need persistence, a primary trait of a super leader according to a California university professor. John Stott declared, "It is one thing to dream dreams and see visions. It is another to convert a dream into a plan of action. It is yet a third to persevere with it when opposition comes, for opposition is bound to arise" (*Involvement*, Vol. 2, p. 255).

Joshua faced many pressures. Some were internal, but most were external. Yet like the Apostle Paul (2 Tim. 4:7), he persevered to the end.

Opposition, it is said, develops strong men, who rise like kites against the wind. This principle is validated in Scripture, with Joshua among the most vivid examples. So, we learn in this book from a leader under fire how to trust God as we face the hard task and how to persevere in the midst of opposition.

Outline of the Book of Joshua

I. The Invasion of Canaan   1:1—5:12
   A. The Commissioning of Joshua   1
   B. The Spying Out of Jericho   2
   C. The Crossing of the Jordan   3
   D. The Erection of Memorials   4
   E. The Consecration of the Israelites   5:1-12

II. The Conquest of Canaan   5:13—12:24
   A. The Central Campaign   6—8
   B. The Southern Campaign   9—10
   C. The Northern Campaign   11:1-15
   D. The Review of the Victories   11:16—12:24

III. The Division of Canaan   13—21
   A. The Portion of the Two-and-One-Half Tribes   13
   B. The Portion of Caleb   14
   C. The Portion of the Nine-and-One-Half Tribes   15:1—19:48
   D. The Portion of Joshua; the Manslayer and the Levites   19:49—21:45

IV. Conclusion   22—24
   A. A Border Dispute   22
   B. The Last Days of Joshua   23—24

1
Facing
a New Day

Joshua 1

"The history of the world is the history of its great men."
The Book of Joshua confronts us with the compelling history
of a dynamic leader—Joshua, son of Nun, and successor to
Moses.

Joshua's preparation for spiritual leadership was long—
such preparation usually is. Josephus, the noted Jewish historian, believed Joshua was 40 years old at the time of the
Exodus. At the age of 80, God's preparation of this man was
completed. He was ready for his task.

Abraham Lincoln was once asked about his ambitions as a
political leader and he replied, "I will prepare myself and be
ready; perhaps my chance will come." Joshua's hour had
come.

The New Leader

Moses was dead and Joshua was about to step into the empty
place. The death of a national leader often precipitates a crisis.
As a college student, I heard the chilling words, "F.D.R. is
dead!" And I anxiously wondered if the Vice-President,
Harry Truman, could pick up the mantle of the fallen leader.
Eighteen years later, I heard a radio announcer grimly say,

"President Kennedy is dead!" Shortly before returning to Washington, Vice-President Johnson was sworn into office.

From the human point of view, the transition from Moses to Joshua was momentous. But the real Leader of Israel, Jehovah, was alive. It was He who now communicated with Joshua.

Joshua Listened to the Lord (1:1-9)

Joshua waited expectantly near the swiftly flowing Jordan River to hear the voice of God, and he was not disappointed. When His servants take time to listen, God always communicates. In our time He speaks through His written Word; then, it was in a dream by night, in a vision by day, through the high priest of the tabernacle, or by an audible voice.

However God communicated with Joshua, the message came loud and clear: Moses was dead, but God's purpose was very much alive, and Joshua was now the key figure to the fulfillment of God's program.

The instructions to Joshua were clear: he was to assume immediate command of all the people and lead them across the Jordan.

For all these centuries, nations have questioned Israel's right to the land which God was about to give them. But no one can question God's right to give Canaan to Israel, for He owns all the lands of Planet Earth. "The earth is the Lord's, and all it contains, the world, and those that dwell in it" (Ps. 24:1).

Although the land was God's gift to Israel, it would only be won by hard fighting. The Lord gave them title to the territory, but they could possess it only by marching on every part. The boundaries were to extend from the wilderness on the south to the Lebanon mountain range on the north; and from the Euphrates River on the east to the Mediterranean Sea on the west.

When Joshua heard these words, his heart must have skipped a beat or two! Thirty-eight years before, as one of the twelve spies sent by Moses, he had walked through this good and fruitful land. (See Numbers 13.) The memory of its beauty and fertility was not dimmed. Now he was to lead the armies of Israel to conquer Canaan.

The territory actually conquered and possessed in the time of Joshua was much less than what had been promised. Even in the time of David and Solomon when the land reached its greatest extent, the outlying districts of what had been promised were within Israel's sphere of influence, but not under its rule.

When will the nation of Israel fully possess the land? In November of 1947, 56 delegates to the United Nations met in Flushing, New York to decide the future of Israel. As the delegate of Guatemala rose to cast the first vote, a piercing cry came from the spectators' gallery, a Hebrew cry as old as the suffering of that people, *"Ana Ad Hoshija."* "O Lord, save us!" The results of the vote were 33 for, 10 against, and 13 abstaining. Jews danced in the streets of New York, Philadelphia, Sao Paulo, London, Paris, Tel Aviv.

In Jerusalem, Golda Meir said, "We have waited 2,000 years for our deliverance." David Ben-Gurion whispered in awe, "At last we are a free people."

But Palestine was still a divided land and Jerusalem a divided city. Not until 1967 was Israel able to expand her territory and unify the city of Jerusalem. But she is far from occupying all that was promised. Tremendous world pressures are being directed to force Israel to return much of her conquered territories to Arab peoples. Resistance against Israel will come to a climax at the time of Christ's return to earth, when He will deliver the Jews and reign in the land over a converted and redeemed Israel. Complete possession of the land awaits that glorious day.

Apathy, unbelief, and disobedience kept the people under Joshua from claiming all that God wanted to give them. And for the same reasons, most Christians fall far short of appropriating the spiritual blessings God has provided them now in Christ. Christians are blessed with "every spiritual blessing in the heavenly places in Christ" (Eph. 1:3), but they possess only what they appropriate.

As Joshua faced the tremendous task of conquering Canaan, he desperately needed a word of encouragement. Joshua knew the Canaanites were vigorous people who lived in strongly fortified cities. Frequent battles kept their warriors in trim fighting condition. Most of their land was mountainous, a fact that would make war maneuvers very difficult.

But God never gives a command without a promise; He assured Joshua of a lifetime of continuous victory over his enemies, based on His unfailing presence and help. The promise "I will not fail you or forsake you" may be translated, "I will not drop or abandon you," or even, "I will not leave you in the lurch." God never walks out on His promises.

Flowing from this strong affirmation came a threefold call to courage.

• Joshua was to be strong and courageous because of the *promise of the land*. Although he would need strength and fortitude for the strenuous military campaign just ahead, Joshua was to keep uppermost in his mind the fact that he would succeed in causing Israel to inherit the land because it had been promised to "their fathers," to Abraham (Gen. 13:14ff; 15:18ff; 17:7ff); to Isaac (Gen. 26:3ff); to Jacob (Gen. 28:13; 35:12), and to the entire nation, the seed of Abraham (Ex. 6:8), as an eternal possession.

Now at last Joshua was to lead the sons of Israel into possession of this Promised Land. What a strategic role he would play at this crucial time in his nation's history!

While fulfillment of this promise to possess and retain the land depends in any given generation on Israel's obedience to God, there can be no question but that the Bible affirms their legal right to the land. By divine contract the title is theirs, even though they will not possess it totally and enjoy it fully until they are right with God.

• Joshua was to be strong and courageous because of the *power of the Word of God.* This exhortation was stronger than the first, indicating that greater strength of character is required to obey God's Word faithfully and fully, than is needed to win military battles! These verses clearly speak of a written body of truth. Although critics argue that the Scriptures did not appear in written form until several centuries later, we read here of an authoritative "Book of the Law."

If Joshua wanted prosperity and success in the conquest of Canaan, and unquestionably he did, he was instructed to observe the following:

• The Law was not to depart out of his mouth; he was to talk about it.

• He was to meditate on it day and night; he was to think about it.

• He was to obey its commands; he was to live according to it.

The record of Joshua's life, as told in the Books of Exodus through Joshua, demonstrates that he lived according to the teachings of the Law of Moses. This alone explains the victories he achieved in battle and the success with which his entire career was marked. In one of his farewell addresses to the nation just prior to his death, he urged the people also to live their lives in submission to the Scriptures (Josh. 23:6). Joshua's generation heeded this charge, but succeeding generations refused to be guided by God's authoritative revelation, choosing rather to do what was right in their own eyes (Jud. 21:25). Rejecting an objective standard of righteousness, they chose to follow the moral and spiritual relativism of a subjective standard. The choice led Israel into centuries of religious apostasy and moral anarchy.

Many secular and religious authorities believe that the United States is similarly headed for disaster. In large measure Western civilization has already rejected the authority of Scripture for moral and spiritual relativism. Former Chief Justice Frederick M. Vinson stated, "Nothing is more certain in modern society than the principle that there are no absolutes."

Francis Schaeffer declared,

Humanists have been determined to beat to death the knowledge of God and the knowledge that God has not been silent, but has spoken in the Bible and through Christ—and they have been determined to do this, even though the death of values has come with the death of that knowledge (*How Should We Then Live?* Revell, p. 226).

We are witnessing the death of biblical values. But with the death of these values will come ultimately the death of civilization. The co-producer of a popular Hollywood movie said recently that movies have taught people, college students especially, that they can do any crazy thing they want to. There are no beliefs to tie people down. (*The Dallas Morning News*, February 8, 1979).

Joshua believed, and so must we, that there is a God to whom we must give account, a God who has revealed Himself and His will for man in the Holy Scriptures. True prosperity and success for the individual and the nation come only by following His teachings.

• Joshua was to be courageous because of *the promised presence of the Lord*. Joshua faced an enormous task—there would be giants and fortified cities, but the presence of God would make all the difference. Martin Luther said, "One plus God equals a majority!"

Joshua probably had times when he felt weak, inadequate, and frightened. But God, knowing all about those feelings of personal weakness and fear, said three times to Joshua, "Be strong and of a good courage." These charges with their accompanying assurances, were sufficient to last a lifetime.

Joshua Commanded His Officers (1:10-15)

The Lord had spoken to Joshua. Now Joshua spoke to the people, and did so without delay. There was a note of certainty about Joshua's commands; the new leader was taking charge with confidence.

Joshua and the people faced a situation that closely paralleled the dilemma Moses and the Israelites faced at the Red Sea (Ex. 14). In each case, the obstacle occurred at the beginning of the leader's ministry. Both were impossible to solve through natural means. Both demanded implicit and absolute dependence upon a miracle-working God.

Two matters had to be taken care of during the three days before the march across the Jordan began. First, provisions had to be gathered; for even though the daily manna had not yet ceased, they were apparently to gather some of the fruit and grain from the plains of Moab for themselves and their cattle. The order to prepare was given by Joshua to his officers, who then issued the orders of the commander to the people.

Joshua attended to the second order of business as he reminded the tribes of Reuben, Gad, and the half-tribe of Manasseh of their commitment to assist in conquering the land west of Jordan. Although they had received their inheritance on the east side of the Jordan, their response showed they were ready to stand by their promise. Joshua had a special mission for them—to serve as shock troops in leading the attack on Canaan.

Joshua Received Support from the People (1:16-18).

The response of the Transjordanian tribes was enthusiastic and wholehearted, and no doubt a profound encouragement to Joshua. Their pledge of loyalty and obedience included the solemn declaration that anyone guilty of disobedience would be executed.

But there was one condition: they were willing to follow Joshua, provided he showed clear evidence that he was being led by God. This was a wise precaution and one that should be carefully followed by all of the Lord's people, or they may find their guides to be "blind leaders of the blind."

A recent tragic example of this kind of leadership was Jim Jones, the cult leader of the People's Temple. His 900 followers committed murder-suicide in Guyana, in November 1978.

Joshua was no "blind leader of the blind." The hand of God was upon him all his days, and with faith in the Lord he moved boldly forward to lead the people in the conquest of the land of promise. What was the secret of Joshua's success? "This Book of the Law shall not depart from your mouth; but you shall meditate on it day and night, so that you may be careful to do according to all that is written in it; for then you will make your way prosperous, and then you will have success" (1:8).

Alan Redpath declares:

I have no magic formula for your holiness; I have no hocus-pocus treatment to offer you; I have no short-cut to spiritual power for any of you. All I can do is to say to you: Get back to your Bible; 'meditate therein day and night,' and go down before God on your face in prayer. For the greatest transactions of a man's experience are made, not in a church, but behind closed doors" (*Victorious Christian Living*, Revell, pp. 32-33).

After being elected president of one of our country's largest insurance companies, the new CEO addressed his entire home office population:

I have some deep spiritual and religious convictions that I've tried to make part of my life. I have a very deep consciousness of the overriding providence of God in the affairs of men. I don't believe that our civilization is automatic. I don't believe our country's blessings are automatic. I don't believe the great prosperity of this company is automatic. I believe we are subject to the overruling providence of God in the affairs of our lives, and I can tell you in these last few days that I spent a lot of time in thankful prayer to God for what He has brought to pass in my life. And I think you ought to know this.

I believe in these things very strongly. I'm not trying to impose anything that I believe or say on anyone else. . . . This is the way I feel about it. . . . I'm just deeply honored and deeply humbled to have this job and to be a part of your organization and to work with you. I again solicit your cooperation and your help (Harold F. Boss, *How Green the Grazing*, Taylor Publishing Co., p. 272).

As the newly appointed Joshua stood before his people, he inspired confidence. Joshua has always been considered one of the great heroes of the Bible because of his sheer courage, and selfless and dynamic leadership.

General Douglas MacArthur once listed Joshua among the few truly great generals of world history. President Theodore Roosevelt often said that the Book of Joshua was his favorite book in the Bible. He frequently referred to the man Joshua in his speeches, and was no doubt motivated by the Old Testament general to be vigorous, forthright, and fearless in his own position of national leadership.

William S. LaSor wrote,

"God expects each generation to get up on its own feet and face its own problems. God does not want us to stand around saying, "Well, now, look at Moses. *There* was a great man! We will never have another man like Moses!" . . . Moses is dead. Great man that he was, he is dead. Get up and face the problems of your day and your age! Arise, go over this Jordan. Do not long for the past. Do the work of the present, and God says, "I will be with you" (*Great Personalities of the Bible*, Revell, p. 77).

2
Living
in Enemy Territory

Joshua 2

Elie Cohn was called Israel's greatest spy. He infiltrated the
highest echelons of the Syrian government, gaining access to
vital military secrets. He even toured military installations on
the Syrian-Israeli border where he learned the defense plans,
the attack plans, and the location of armaments and fortifica-
tions. All of this he reported to Israel by a hidden transmitter
in Damascus, and thereby helped Israel achieve one of its most
outstanding victories on June 5, 1967.

This dramatic and unforgettable story has its prototype in
the thrilling adventure of the two spies sent out by Joshua
to penetrate the Canaanite society and bring back vital information.

It is well known that the function of the spy in war is
a dangerous one; yet it is absolutely necessary. Everything depends on the commander of an army having
accurate intelligence of the position and movement of
the enemy, if they are in the field; or of the strength,
character, and position of the fortification, if it is a city
that is to be attacked. The work of a spy demands great
courage, coolness, adroitness, and resource. If he is found
out, he is shot without mercy (George Hague, *Practical*

Studies in the History and Biography of the Old Testament, Witness Printing House, p. 11).

Joshua too had been a spy. Now as he faced westward and viewed the land of God's promise across the turbulent Jordan, it was natural that he should take steps to secure the kind of information necessary for the success of the first battle in what promised to be a long and difficult war.

The Spies Were Sent to Jericho (2:1)

The walled city of Jericho stood in the path the Israeli invaders would take. Jericho was the key citadel of the Jordan Valley, and commanded passes into the central highlands. Before his army attacked, Joshua needed complete information concerning this fortress—its gates, fortified towers, military force, and the morale of its people. Two secret agents were chosen and sent on a carefully concealed mission. Not even the Israelites were to know; Joshua didn't want an unfavorable report to dishearten them, as it had their fathers at Kadesh-Barnea (Num. 13:28—14:4).

Taking their lives in their hands, the two spies left Shittim, some six miles east of the Jordan, and probably traveled north, swimming across the flooded river at some fords. Turning south, they approached Jericho and soon were moving along its streets, mingling with the people.

We are not told how the spies chose the house of Rahab the harlot. While some writers suggest they saw her walking the streets and followed her, I believe that God led the men to her house. God's purpose for the spies included more than the securing of military information. There was in Jericho a sinful woman whom God in grace purposed to spare from the judgment soon to fall on the city. So the Lord, moving in mysterious ways, brought together two secret agents of the army of Israel and a harlot of Canaan who would become a proselyte to the God of Israel.

Historians from the time of Josephus to the present have attempted to soften the situation by arguing that Rahab was only an innkeeper. But New Testament references (Heb. 11:31 and James 2:25) support the conclusion that she was an immoral woman. This in no way impugns the righteousness of God—that He would use such a person in the fulfillment of His purposes—but brings into bold relief His mercy and grace. (See Matt. 21:32; Luke 15:1; 19:10.)

Nor should we infer that the spies visited Rahab for immoral purposes. William Blaikie wrote:

The emissaries of Joshua were in too serious peril, in too devout a mood, and in too high-strung a state of nerve to be at the mercy of any Delilah that might wish to lure them to careless pleasure. Their faith, their honor, their patriotism, and their regard to their leader Joshua, all demanded the extremist circumspection and self-control; they were, like Peter, walking on the sea; unless they kept their eye on their Divine Protector, their courage and presence of mind would fail them; they would be at the mercy of their foes (*The Book of Joshua*, Hodder & Stoughton, p. 85).

The Spies Were Shielded by Rahab (2:2-7)

The entire city of Jericho was on alert, knowing about the camp of Israel opposite them across the Jordan. Someone detected the agents, followed them to Rahab's house, and quickly returned to report to the king. The king quickly sent messengers who demanded that Rahab surrender the spies. In keeping with oriental custom, the privacy of even a woman like Rahab was respected, and the king's men refrained from bursting into her house to prosecute their search.

Rahab had her own suspicions about the identity of the two visitors. When she saw the soldiers approaching her house, she hid the spies beneath the stalks of flax which were drying on her flat roof.

When she opened her front door to the king's messengers, she freely admitted that two strangers had come to her house—but how was she to know their identity and mission? "They left here at dusk, just about the time the city gate is closed. But if you hurry you can probably catch them!" The soldiers took Rahab at her word, made no search of her property, and quickly set out on a wild-goose chase due east to the fords of the Jordan, the most likely escape route.

Was it wrong for Rahab to lie, since her falsehood protected the spies? Are there some situations in which a lie is acceptable?

After all, some say this was a cultural matter, for Rahab was born and raised among the depraved Canaanites who thought nothing of lying. She probably saw no evil in her act. Further, if she had told the truth, the spies would surely have been killed by the king of Jericho.

But such arguments are not all that convincing. Pastor Erwin Lutzer describes a situation which logically seemed to call for lying, but which in the end brought worse results than would have come from the truth.

Several years ago the State Department lied about the U-2 spy plane incident. This may have been done out of love for 180 million Americans, because their trust in the honesty of the government is crucial. Also it preserved good relations with Russia and kept a military secret which was necessary to insure future security measures. Although the original explanation by the State Department was plausible, the lie was discovered. This resulted in greater hatred among nations, and the confidence of many Americans was lost (*The Morality Gap*, Moody Press, p. 55).

To argue that the spies would certainly have perished if Rahab had been truthful is to ignore the option that God could have protected the spies in some other way. To excuse Rahab for indulging in a common practice is to condone what God condemns. Paul quoted a poet of Crete who said that Cretans were inveterate liars, and then added, "This testimony is true. For this cause reprove them severely that they may be sound in the faith" (Titus 1:13). The lie of Rahab was recorded but not approved. The Bible approves her faith, demonstrated by good works, but not her falsehood.

The Spies Were Given Intelligence Information (2:8-11)

After the king's messengers went away, Rahab climbed to the roof of her home where she talked with the two spies in the darkness. They could hardly have been prepared for the declarations of her faith which followed. First, she disclosed that she believed that the Lord, the God of Israel, had given them the land of Canaan. Though the army of Israel had not yet crossed the Jordan River, Rahab stated in effect, "The conquest is as good as over."

Second, she revealed the priceless information to the spies that the inhabitants of Jericho, as well as of the rest of Canaan, were utterly demoralized. Since a major objective of the spy mission was to assess the morale of the enemy, this word was indeed welcome news. But why the terror? Because of the power of Israel's God, power which parted the Red Sea for the Hebrew slaves 40 years before, and more recently gave them victories over the mighty kings of the Amorites east of the Jordan, Sihon, and Og. Now that same divine power was closing in on the residents of Jericho, and they knew they could not resist.

Rahab knew better than to believe that a nation of former slaves could have achieved such feats by their own strength, and resources.

She was no philosopher, and could not have reasoned on the doctrine of causation, but her common sense taught her that you cannot have extraordinary effects without corresponding causes.

It is one of the great weaknesses of modern unbelief that with all its pretensions to philosophy, it is constantly accepting effects without adequate cause: Jesus Christ, though He revolutionized the world, though He founded an empire to which that of the Caesars is not for a moment to be compared, though all that were about Him admitted His supernatural power and Person, after all, was nothing but a man. The Gospel that has brought peace and joy to so many weary hearts, that has transformed the slaves of sin into children of heaven, that has turned cannibals into saints, and fashioned so many an angelic character out of the rude blocks of humanity, is but a cunningly devised fable.

What contempt for such sophistries . . . would this poor woman have shown! How does she rebuke the many that keep pottering in poor natural explanations of plain supernatural facts, instead of manfully admitting that it is the arm of God that has been revealed, and the voice of God that has spoken" (Blaikie, *The Book of Joshua*, pp. 87-88).

Finally, Rahab declared her faith in Israel's God: "For the Lord your God, He is God in heaven above and on earth beneath." Responding to the word she had received about the mighty working of God, Rahab believed. She trusted in God's power and mercy, and that faith saved her.

The Spies Promised Protection for Rahab (2:12-21).
Not only did Rahab demonstrate her faith by the protection of the spies, but also by her concern for the safety of her family. Admittedly, it was their physical deliverance that she sought. But it is not farfetched to see in this also her further desire that they too from this time on be a part of God's people, serving the one true God of Israel instead of being enslaved to the vile and degrading idolatry of the Canaanites.

She pursued this urgent matter delicately but persistently, pressing the spies to make a pact with her because of her cooperation with them.

When Rahab asked for "kindness" to be shown to her family, she used a significant and meaningful word, *hesed*. Found some 250 times in the Old Testament, *hesed* means loyal, steadfast, or faithful love based on an unwritten promise, agreement or covenant. Sometimes, the word is used for God's covenant love for His people; and sometimes, as here, for relationships on the human level. Rahab's request then was that the spies make a *hesed* agreement with her and her father's house, just as she had made a *hesed* agreement with them by sparing their lives.

The response of the spies was immediate and decisive. "When the Lord gives us the land, we will keep the *hesed* agreement. If you do not report our mission, we will protect you and your family or forfeit our own lives!" (See v. 14.)

As the spies prepared to go, they again confirmed the desperate pact by repeating and enlarging the conditions Rahab must abide by.

• First, her house must be designated by a scarlet cord hung from the window. Because of the position of the house on the wall, the cord would be clearly seen by the Israelite soldiers again and again as they would march around the walls. Her home would be clearly marked so that no soldier, however fierce and eager he might be in the work of destruction, would dare violate the oath and kill its inhabitants.

• Second, Rahab and her family were to remain in the house during the attack on Jericho. If anyone of them wandered out and was killed, the responsibility for his death would be his own.

• Finally, the spies again emphasized that they would be free of this oath of protection if Rahab exposed their mission.

It is not hard to imagine Rahab hurrying to gather her family in her house on the city wall. The door of her house was a door to safety from the judgment soon to fall on Jericho.

In the days of Noah, there was safety for those who entered the door of the ark; in Egypt there was freedom from judgment for those gathered inside the doors sprinkled with the blood of the Passover lamb.

Jesus said, "I am the door; if anyone enters through Me, he shall be saved" (John 10:9). Safety from eternal judgment depends on entering the right door!

George Whitefield, the eloquent preacher of the Great

Awakening in North America (1738-1740), was speaking once on the text, "The door was shut." There were two flippant young men in the congregation, and one was overhead to say to the other in sarcastic tones, "What if the door is shut? Another will open!"

Later in the sermon the evangelist said, "It is possible that there may be someone here who is careless and trifling, and says: 'What matter if the door be shut? Another will open!' "

The two young men looked at each other in alarm. Mr. Whitefield proceeded, "Yes, another door will open. It will be the door to the bottomless pit—the door to hell!"

The Spies Returned to Joshua (2:22-24)
Their mission completed, the spies exchanged parting instructions with Rahab, concerning their escape and return to Joshua. Jericho at this time was surrounded by two walls about 15 feet apart. Planks of wood spanned the gap and then houses were built on this foundation. Probably due to lack of space in the small city, Rahab's house was one of those built on the wall. So the spies were carefully lowered by rope from a window of Rahab's house. Escape would have been much more difficult, had it had been necessary for them to go out the city gate.

Scarcely a half-mile west of Jericho are limestone cliffs about 1,500 feet high, honeycombed with caves; and here the spies hid out until the soldiers of Jericho gave up the hunt. Then, under cover of darkness, the spies swam back across the Jordan, making their way quickly to the camp at Shittim, to present their report to Joshua. How excited they must have been to relate their strange and stirring adventure, and to report the alarm and utter despondency of the Canaanites. Their conclusion was, "Surely the *Lord* has given all the land into our hands." How different from the report of the majority of the spies at Kadesh-Barnea who said, "We are not able to go up against the people, for they are too strong for us" (Num. 13:31).

Joshua received the news with gratitude to God. Early the next morning, he organized the army of Israel for the attack on Jericho.

While the two young spies and their remarkable exploits are not to be minimized, Rahab's supporting role leaves lasting and even deeper impressions. Whenever she is spoken of in the Bible, she is referred to as a harlot. This is not to humiliate her or to demean her memory, but to cast in bold relief the grace of God that saved her. Regardless of the kind of life a person has lived, there is forgiveness for sin and eternal life available in Jesus Christ.

John Newton had a similarly remarkable conversion. Losing his mother when he was seven years old, he went to sea at the age of eleven. "I went to Africa," he said, "that I might be free to sin to my heart's content." And that he did!

During the next few years, Newton's soul was seared by the most revolting of all human experiences. He fell into the pitiless clutches of the press-gang. Later as a deserter from the navy, he was flogged until the blood streamed down his back. He became involved in the unspeakable atrocities of the African slave trade. And then, going from bad to worse, he actually became a slave himself. He was sold to a woman slave who, glorying in her power over him, made him depend for his food upon the crusts she tossed under her table. In the epitaph that he composed for himself, Newton said that he was "the slave of the slaves."

And then it happened! In 1748, on board a ship about to founder in the grips of a storm, the Lord came from on high and delivered him out of deep waters. When the ship went plunging down into the trough of the seas, few on board expected her to come up again. As Newton hurried to the pumps, he said to the captain, "If this will not do, the Lord have mercy upon us!" His own words startled him. "Mercy!" he said to himself in astonishment. "Mercy! Mercy!" On the 10th of March 1748, Newton sought mercy—and found it!

The Bible emphasizes not only that Rahab was saved by

faith, but also that she demonstrated her faith by her works: she protected the spies, she dropped the scarlet thread from her window, and she gathered her family in her house to protect them from the judgment to fall on Jericho. Rahab took her life in her hands to protect the spies; she believed God even though she had limited knowledge of Him (Heb. 11:6).

Francis Schaeffer puts it well:

This woman Rahab stood alone in faith against the *total* culture which surrounded her—something none of us today in the Western world has ever yet had to do. For a period of time she stood for the unseen against the seen, standing in acute danger until Jericho fell. If the king had ever found out what she had done, he would have become her chief enemy and would have executed her. . . . This is exactly how the Christian lives, and Rahab is a tremendous example for us. Though you and I have stepped from the kingdom of darkness into the kingdom of God's dear Son, we are still surrounded by a culture controlled by God's great enemy, Satan. We must live in it from the moment we accept Christ as Saviour until judgment falls. We too are encompassed by one who was once our king but is now our enemy. It is just plain stupid of a Christian not to expect spiritual warfare while he lives in enemy territory" (*Joshua and the Flow of Biblical History*, Inter-Varsity Press, pp. 79-80).

Living in enemy territory is dangerous and demands a vital faith in the living God. Rahab possessed it and demonstrated it. Do you?

3
Fording
Uncrossable Rivers

Joshua 3-4

"The difficult we will do immediately; the impossible may take us a while longer!" Following this slogan, battalions of courageous and hardworking men called Seabees followed combat units into newly conquered territories during World War II, to build barracks, bridges, roads, and landing strips.

Israel might have desired the same human assistance. But accompanying Israel's army, to enable them to do the impossible, was God Himself; and Israel needed the assurance of His presence. After 40 years of wandering in the desert, thinking they had at last come to their own homeland, they faced what appeared to be an insurmountable difficulty.

Life is like that. Sometimes when hopes are the highest, problems suddenly appear which are as formidable to us as the swirling waters of the Jordan were to the Israelites.

After hearing a message at a Bible conference on how to cope with discouragement, three people greeted the speaker: a young mother who had not slept the previous night because her husband had come home at 10:30 P.M. and announced he was divorcing her; a pastor whose teenage daughter was rebelling against God; and a Christian worker whose husband had entered the hospital for treatment of a brain tumor.

Stated a pastor, "The trouble is that we are facing problems that *we* cannot solve: this customer I must sell, that exam I must take, this debt I must pay, those in-laws I must endure, that habit I must break, this marriage I must save."

And many have passed the breaking point. Nearly 700,000 Americans are now in mental institutions, with that number rapidly increasing. It is predicted that 15 million Americans will experience nervous breakdowns in their lifetimes. More than 100,000 attempt suicide every year and 3 million are disabled by alcohol annually. The narcotics casualties are almost innumerable.

It has been said that the only difference between a live wire and a dead one is the connection. A supernatural source of strength is available in every generation to enable God's children to cross the rivers of impossibility.

Preparations for the Crossing (3:1-4)

Joshua was a man of action. On the basis of the spies' report, he began immediate preparations to cross the Jordan and invade Canaan. He had no knowledge of how this large group of people was to cross the swollen river, but he believed that God would somehow make it possible. And so he moved them all, bag and baggage, the seven miles from Shittim to the Jordan.

When the time came to actually move toward Jordan, Joshua did not request an extension of time in order to let the Jordan subside. He did not plead for a different route so as to avoid confrontation with the enemy. He did not call for a caucus, a commission, or a committee report in five copies with this committee to be duly organized and named "The Committee on Crisis in the Contemporary Situation" (John J. Davis, *Conquest and Crisis*, Baker, p. 35).

When they arrived at the river, they stopped for three days. Why the delay? Time was no doubt needed for the leaders to organize the crossing and pass instructions on to the people. The delay also allowed them an opportunity to get close and see the river, now a strong and rapid current due to the melting of the winter snows of Mt. Hermon in the north. The people must have wondered: "How does Joshua expect us to cross?"

At the end of the third day of waiting, Joshua gave the instructions: The pillar of cloud would no longer lead them, but they were instead to follow the Ark of the Covenant. Priests bearing the Ark would advance first into the land. And since the Ark symbolized the Lord Himself, it was Jehovah who led His people into Canaan. "Behold the Ark of the Covenant of the Lord of all the earth is crossing over ahead of you into the Jordan" (3:11).

With the Ark going ahead, the people would fall in behind, or spread around it on three sides; but they were to keep a distance of 3,000 feet. Why? To remind them of the sacredness of the Ark and the holiness of the God it represented. There was to be no casual nor careless intimacy, but a profound spirit of respect and reverence. God is not "the man upstairs," but the sovereign and holy Lord of all the earth.

The distance was also essential so that the largest possible number in this great population could observe the Ark. God was about to lead them over unfamiliar ground, over a way they had not taken previously. It was new territory; and without the guidance and leadership of the Lord, the people would not know which direction to take.

"It is reassuring for a Christian to know that God is with him when his path carries him over new territory—sickness, pain, bereavement, failure, financial difficulties, misunderstanding, opposition. In times like these, believers may hear the Lord's voice saying. 'Be of good courage! Fear not!' " (*Bible Knowledge*, Scripture Press, April 1963, p. 39)

The Israelites were about to experience God's loving intervention on their behalf.

Consecration for the Crossing (3:5-13)
As the day for the crossing approached, Joshua commanded the people to sanctify themselves. Most military leaders would

have said, "Sharpen your swords and polish your shields!" But for the people of God, it was spiritual rather than military preparation that was most essential at this time, for God was about to reveal Himself by performing a great miracle in Israel's midst! And just as we would prepare scrupulously to meet someone of earthly fame, so it was appropriate for the Israelites to prepare for a manifestation of the God of all the earth. The same command was heard at Sinai by the previous generation, as they prepared themselves for the majestic revelation of Jehovah in the giving of the Law (Ex. 19:10).

On the night of his graduation from medical school, Dr. Howard A. Kelly, later a world-famous surgeon, wrote in his diary: "I dedicate myself, my time, my capabilities, my ambition, everything to Him. Blessed Lord, sanctify me to Thy uses. Give me no worldly success which may not lead me nearer to my Saviour!"

For spiritual victory we too must be willing to separate ourselves from defiling sin, so that we can be set apart to God's will and purpose for our lives. This was Israel's challenge and it is ours.

But that is not all. The people of Israel were to *expect* God to work a miracle. They were to be eager, gripped by a sense of wonder. Said one writer, "It is because we lose sight of a God who can do the incredible and the impossible that we meet frustration and futility."

The Lord then revealed to Joshua the means of the crossing, so that he in turn could explain the same to the people. And the Lord explained to Joshua that this miracle would magnify or exalt him as the leader of the people. It was time to establish the credential of Joshua as God's representative to guide Israel. What better way to accomplish this than for Joshua to direct their passage through a miraculously parted river? After the crossing it was recorded, "On that day the Lord exalted Joshua in the sight of all Israel; so that they revered him, just as they had revered Moses all the days of his life."

But when Joshua passed on the words of God to the people,

he did not disclose the special promise that he would be exalted by this miraculous event. Rather he told them it would certify that the living God, in contrast to the dead idols worshiped by the heathen, was in their midst. Furthermore, the living God would not only open a way across the flooded Jordan, but would also drive out the seven tribes inhabiting the land.

"The living God is among you!" This became the watchword of the conquest, the key to victory over the enemies of the land. God's promise—"I will be with you!"—appears on almost every page of the Book of Joshua. It is a promise of His presence that still sustains the Lord's people.

During the Civil War, the town of Moresfield, West Virginia was on the dividing line, and seesawed back and forth between Federal and Confederate troops. In one old house which still stands today, an elderly woman lived alone. One morning Yankee troops stomped up on her porch. Though at their mercy, she remained calm and invited them to be seated at her table.

When breakfast was set before them, she said, "It is a custom of long standing in this house to have prayers before meals. I hope you won't mind." With that, she picked up the Bible, opened it at random and began to read from Psalm 27 (KJV):

The Lord is my Light and my Salvation; whom shall I fear? The Lord is the Strength of my life; of whom shall I be afraid? When the wicked, even mine enemies and my foes, came upon me to eat up my flesh, they stumbled and fell. Though an host should encamp against me, my heart shall not fear; though war should rise against me, in this will I be confident. . . . I had fainted, unless I had believed to see the goodness of the Lord in the land of the living! Wait on the Lord; be of good courage, and He shall strengthen thine heart, wait, I say, on the Lord.

When she finished, she murmured quietly, "Let us pray." As she prayed, she heard stealthy sounds of shuffling shoes. When she ended with "Amen," she opened her eyes. The soldiers were gone! Her lack of fear had made them fearful of lingering any longer!

Completion of the Crossing (3:14-17)

The day to cross the Jordan, the day when Israel was to enter Canaan, finally arrived. The people folded their tents and followed the Ark-bearing priests to the brink of the Jordan. It was the time of the barley harvest, the month of Nisan (March-April). The river was brimful, a foreboding sight to the priests and a severe test of their faith. Would they hesitate in fear or would they advance in faith believing that what God had promised would come to pass?

The priests were not expected to act on blind faith—nor are we. Their faith and ours is based on what God has revealed, on what He has promised.

"What do you do with the promises of God?" someone asked.

"I underline them in blue," was the reply. Like the priests at the Jordan, we must do much more. We must appropriate them by faith and make them our own!

Dramatic things happened when priests carrying the Ark of the Covenant stepped into the muddy, swirling waters: "The water from upstream stopped flowing. It piled up in a heap a great distance away, at a town called Adam in the vicinity of Zarethan, while the water flowing down to the Sea of Arabah (the Salt Sea) was completely cut off. So the people crossed over opposite Jericho." (3:16, NIV).

While the place-name Adam is found only here, it is usually identified with Tell ed-Damiyeh, some 16 miles above the ford opposite Jericho. A wide stretch of riverbed therefore was dried up, allowing the people with their animals and baggage to hurry across.

How could such a sensational event occur? Many insist the supposed miracle has a natural explanation, pointing out that an earthquake on December 8, 1267 caused the high banks of the Jordan to collapse near ed-Damiyeh damming the river for some 10 hours. On July 11, 1927, another earthquake near the same location caused the blocking of the river for 21 hours. Of course these stoppages did not occur during flood season.

Admittedly, God could have employed a natural cause, and the timing would have still made it a miraculous intervention. But did He? Does the biblical text allow for such an interpretation of this event?

Considering all of the factors involved, it appears best to view this occurrence as a special act of God brought about in a way unknown to us. There were many supernatural elements brought together:

- The event came to pass as predicted.
- The timing was exact.
- The event took place when the river was at flood stage.
- The wall of water was held in place for what was probably an entire day.
- The soft river bottom became dry at once.
- The waters returned immediately as soon as the crossing was completed and the priests came up out of the river. It would be appropriate to ask those who insist on a natural explanation if two earthquakes were required in rather quick sequence to part the Jordan for the Prophets Elijah and Elisha to cross (2 Kings 2:8, 14).

In the crossing of the Jordan River at floodstage by a nation some two million strong, God was glorified, Joshua was exalted, and Israel was encouraged. But the Canaanites were terrorized.

The crossing of the Jordan meant that Israel was irrevocably committed to a struggle against armies, chariots, and fortified cities. They were also committed to walking by faith in the living God and to turning from a walk according to the flesh, as they had often experienced in the wilderness.

For believers today, a symbolic crossing of the Jordan represents passing from one level of the Christian life to another. It is a picture of entering into spiritual warfare to claim what God has promised. And it should mean the end of life lived by the principle of human effort and the beginning of life lived by the principles of faith and obedience.

The Jordan was the obstacle that kept Israel from the Promised Land. It was the river of impossibility. We also face obstacles that keep us from enjoying a life of faith, obedience, victory. Even if these obstacles appear as formidable as the swirling waters of the Jordan, we must never lose sight of the God who is able to take us through. He has promised, "When you pass through the waters, I will be with you; and through the rivers, they will not overflow you" (Isa. 43:2).

Got any rivers you think are uncrossable?
Got any mountains you can't tunnel through?
God specializes in things thought impossible;
He'll do what no other friend can do.

Memorials of the Crossing (4:1-24)

It was important that this great miracle never be forgotten. So that the Israelites would remember how God acted on their behalf on this historic day, God directed the erection of stone memorials.

Men have always built monuments to memorialize the achievements of man. We think of the Arches of Constantine and Titus in Rome, the Arch of Triumph in Paris, the Washington Arch in New York City, the memorial at Arlington National Cemetery depicting the raising of the U.S. flag on Iwo Jima, the scores of memorials to courageous soldiers on the Civil War battlefields of Vicksburg, Chattanooga, Chickamauga, Manassas and Gettysburg. On the Golan Heights, a striking memorial has been erected to honor the achievements of Israel's fallen sons. All of these serve to remind successive generations of past historical events and great human accomplishments.

But where are the monuments to magnify the greatness and goodness of God? This story describes just such a memorial celebrating the crossing of the Israelite multitudes over the dry riverbed of the Jordan when that stream was at flood stage. Joshua was told by the Lord to direct 12 previously chosen men to carry 12 stones from the bed of the river to the place of the next night's encampment.

Calling the tribal representatives together, Joshua told them that they were to return to the riverbed to secure stones for the memorial which would be a vivid reminder of God's work of deliverance, and an effective medium to teach the young.

The response of the 12 men was immediate and unquestioning. They could well have feared to reenter the Jordan. After all, how long would it remain dry? Whatever fears they may have had were put aside as they unhesitatingly obeyed God's instructions.

Joshua joined the men on their strange mission; and while they were each wrenching up a great stone from the bed of the river, he was moved to set another pile of 12 stones to mark the precise spot where the priests stood with the Ark of the Covenant. This was apparently done on Joshua's own initiative, and expressed his desire to have a personal reminder of God's faithfulness at the very beginning of the conquest of Canaan.

All that the Lord commanded was now accomplished. In anticipation of the Jordan flowing again, the details of the crossing were reviewed:

- The priests and Ark remained in the riverbed while the people hurried across.
- The men of the Transjordanian tribes, not hampered with families and goods, led the crossing.
- When all had crossed and the special mission of the memorials had been completed, the priests left the riverbed and resumed their position at the head of the people.
- The Jordan resumed its flow.

Can you imagine what it must have been like as the Israelites stood on the riverbank watching as the hurrying torrent covered up their path, and then lifting their eyes to look at the opposite side where they had stood that morning? There was no returning now. A new and exciting chapter in their history had begun.

But this was not the time for reflection. Joshua led the people to Gilgal, their first encampment in Canaan, about two miles from Jericho. There the stones taken out of the Jordan were set up, perhaps in a small circle. The name *Gilgal* means "circle."

The purpose of placing the stones was to remind Israel for generations to come that it was God who had brought them through the Jordan, just as He had taken their fathers through the Red Sea.

But how were the future generations to know the significance of the stones? Joshua said to the Israelites,

When your children ask their fathers in time to come, saying, "What are these stones?" Then you shall inform your children, saying, "Israel crossed this Jordan on dry ground." For the Lord your God dried up the waters of the Jordan before you until you had crossed, just as the Lord your God had done to the Red Sea (vv. 21-23).

Parents are to be teachers of God's ways and works to their children (Deut. 6:4-9). Alexander Maclaren, outstanding Bible student and preacher of 19th-century England, said it well:

The Jewish father was not to send his child to some Levite or other to get his question answered, but was to answer it himself. I am afraid that a good many English parents, who call themselves Christians, are too apt to say, "Ask your Sunday School teacher," when such questions are put to them. The decay of parental religious teaching is working enormous mischief in Christian households; and the happiest results would follow if Joshua's homely advice were attended to, "Ye shall let your children know" (*Expositions of Holy Scripture*, III, p. 122).

What an appropriate and timely challenge this is! Christian parents have absolutely no right to abdicate their God-given responsibility to teach their children concerning the faithfulness and power of God. If anything, such teaching is more urgently necessary today than ever before. Satan is doing everything he can to convince young people that God is not essential, and the media may well be his most effective tool. If parents do not counter with biblical teaching, they will lose their children.

The memorial stones had yet another purpose, "that all the peoples of the earth may know that the hand of the Lord is mighty". Thus, as the families of Israel spent their first night in the land, their hearts may well have been filled with uncertainty and fear. The mountains rising steeply to the west looked foreboding. But as the people looked at the 12 stones out of the Jordan, they were reminded that God had done something great for them that day. Surely they could trust Him for the days ahead.

The Lord often works in just this way, giving us experiences in the early days of our Christian lives we can later remember. Then when the storm breaks, we can look back and be reminded of how God worked, and be encouraged to trust Him for the future. Such reminders can be a great testimony to our families and to the world of God's power and faithfulness.

In the history of Dallas Seminary, there are just such "memorial stones." More than 40 years ago, Mrs. Howard Taylor told one such story in a pamphlet entitled, "Empty Racks and How to Fill Them."

In the spring of 1924, plans were being laid for a new seminary to be organized in Dallas, to emphasize above all else the teaching of the Bible itself. Lewis Sperry Chafer, president-elect, had gone to Dundee, Scotland to hold evangelistic meetings at the invitation of a leading manufacturer of that city, in whose home he was a guest. Related Dr. Chafer:

At four o'clock on a never-to-be-forgotten morning, I wakened with a sense of deep foreboding with regard to the agreement reached in Dallas. It seemed as if an unbearable burden had been thrust upon me. Failure, probable if not certain, was the only thing I could see, and all the forebodings the powers of darkness could devise came rolling like billows over me.

In great agony of spirit, I cried to God, saying I could

not go through the day without some very definite indication of His will in the matter. If such indication were not
given, I should have to cable to Dallas requesting them to
discontinue the whole project.

Following that prayer I fell asleep, and later, seated by
my host at the breakfast table, was surprised by his asking whether we had any provision in view for the library
which would be needed for the new seminary. I told him
that we had not, but that since Dr. Griffith Thomas had
just died—whose loss we were mourning on both sides of
the Atlantic—I had written to our constituency in Dallas
asking them to pray definitely that his valuable reference
library might be secured for the college.

"I am interested in what you have told me," he replied,
"and would like you to purchase these books and send the
bill to me. And do not drive too close a bargain; I wish to
pay whatever the library is worth."

A little later that same morning, I had retired to the
study when my host came in and said, "Speaking of the
College, what about your salary as President?" I at once
told him that I had not expected to draw any salary; that
nothing was further from my thoughts.

"You will need some financial help," he replied, "and
though I cannot give all that would be expected for one in
such a position in the United States, I wish to send you
personally two thousand dollars a year."

Truly my cup ran over! The gift of a library valued at
four thousand dollars, and such unexpected provision for
my salary—all in one day! Could I doubt that God desired the Evangelical Theological College to go forward?

Today let us be reminded of some great thing God has done
for us, and let us renew our faith and trust in Him, as we approach an uncertain future.

4
Consecration
Before Conquest

Joshua 5

The Allied invasion of France across the English Channel took place on June 6, 1944. Involved in this immense manuever were 5,300 ships, 12,000 planes, 6 infantry divisions, 14,000 vehicles, 14,500 tons of supplies—all for the purpose of establishing a secure beachhead in enemy-held territory.

The Germans knew a crisis was imminent. On June 3, German intelligence warned that invasion was possible "within the next fortnight."

Casualties numbered in the thousands; but by the end of June the beachhead was established in Normandy, and the Allied armies were striking hard against the enemy across France.

Under Joshua's leadership and by miraculous intervention, some two million soldiers and civilians crossed the Jordan. A beachhead was quickly established at Gilgal, and from every human point of view, it was time to strike the strongholds of Canaan. The morale of the Canaanites had utterly collapsed in the face of the news that was spreading through the land:

- The God of Israel dried up the Red Sea.
- The Israelites defeated the powerful kings of the Amorites in Transjordan.

- Jehovah also dried up the waters of the Jordan so that the Israelites could cross over into Canaan.

Certainly the military leaders of Israel must have favored an immediate all-out offensive. What better time than this to strike a paralyzing blow?

But this was not God's plan. He is never in a hurry, although His children sometimes are. If you feel pressured to make a decision or to act immediately in a situation, without time to consult the Lord about it, you need to resist the pressure. God does not ask you to reach decisions without adequate opportunity for prayer and consideration.

From God's point of view, Israel was not yet ready to fight on the soil of Canaan. There was some unfinished business—and it was spiritual in character. For consecration must precede conquest!

During the German bombings of England in World War II, an Englishman wrote the following in a letter:

As one man,. the whole nation has handed over all its resources to the Government. We have invested the Cabinet with the right to conscript any of us for any task, to take our goods, our money, our all. Never have rich men set such little store by their wealth; never have we been so ready to lay down life itself, if only our cause may triumph.

This is the kind of response God sought from Israel before He would give them the victory. To achieve the response, He led them through four experiences:

- the renewal of circumcision;
- the celebration of the Passover;
- the appropriation of Canaan's produce;
- the acknowledgment of their divine Commander.

The Renewal of Circumcision (5:2-9)

While the surrounding nations were filled with terror, the Lord commanded Joshua to circumcise the sons of Israel. And he obeyed, even though it must have been difficult for him as a military commander to incapacitate his entire army in such an environment.

The men of Israel, who had been circumcised in Egypt, had all died in the wilderness, because of their disobedience at Kadesh-barnea. The sons born during the wilderness wanderings were not circumcised; and it was this new generation upon whom the sacred rite would be performed.

Since the Israelites were slaves in Egypt, they did not practice circumcision until they were about to leave. The Egyptians performed circumcision and would probably have prohibited the practice to the Israelites, since it was reserved for Egyptian priests and upper-class citizens. The Lord acknowledged the completed circumcisions with the declaration, "Today I have rolled away the reproach of Egypt from you."

Further indication of the importance of this event is the fact that a new significance was attached to the name *Gilgal*. Not only was the meaning "circle" to remind Israel of the memorial stones, but now the related idea of "rolling away" would commemorate Israel's act of obedience at the same site.

Why was circumcision so important? Stephen, in his dynamic speech before the Sanhedrin, declared that God gave to Abraham "the covenant of circumcision" (Acts 7:8). Circumcision was no ordinary religious rite, but was rooted in the Abrahamic covenant, a contract guaranteeing the everlasting continuation of Abraham's seed and their everlasting possession of the land. In this connection God designated circumcision as the sign or symbol of that contract, and instructed Abraham that every male person of his household as well as every male child yet to be born was to be circumcised (Gen. 17:7-8, 23-27).

The act of circumcision itself spoke of separation from the widely prevalent sins of the time. Furthermore, the rite had spiritual overtones, not only in relation to sexual conduct, but in every phase of life. "Circumcise then your heart, and stiffen your neck no more" (Deut. 10:16). (See also Deut. 30.6 and Jer. 4:4.)

The Israelites of Joshua's time needed to know that circumcision was not simply a mark in the flesh; there was to be holiness in their lives as well. And this is why at Gilgal, God said in effect, "Before I fight your battles in Canaan, you must have this mark of the covenant in your flesh." Joshua understood the cruciality of this divine requirement and led the people in unhesitating obedience.

Of special interest to us as Christians is the fact that Paul affirmed we have been circumcised in Christ (Col. 2:11). This circumcision is spiritual and relates to our inward beings. This spiritual circumcision takes place at the time of salvation when the Holy Spirit joins the believer to Christ. At that time, the "body of the flesh" or whole carnal nature is judged. As Christians we are to recognize this reality, even though our carnal nature remains a part of us in this life. Our responsibility and privilege is to treat it as a condemned enemy who does not deserve favors.

General Wainwright suffered greatly in a Manchurian prison camp after the fall of Bataan. Japanese prison guards mocked him and made his life totally miserable until he became a broken, crushed, starving man. One day an airplane landed nearby and a colonel of the Allied forces reported to General Wainwright, telling him that Japan had been defeated. Shortly after the colonel left, the prison guards, unaware of what had happened, returned to harass the general as before. This time he retorted, "I am in command here now, and these are my orders!" The guards, shocked speechless, understood that their prisoner had been informed of the Allied victory. From that moment General Wainwright was in supreme command over a defeated enemy.

The Celebration of the Passover (5:10)
Camped at Gilgal, Israel now observed the Passover. Without circumcision they would have been disqualified from the feast (Ex. 12:44, 48).

This was only the third Passover recorded in the Bible. The

first was observed in Egypt in anticipation of their deliverance from bondage and oppression (Ex. 12:1-20). The second was observed at Sinai, just before the people broke camp and moved toward Canaan (Num. 9:5).

There is no indication that the Passover was observed during the wilderness wanderings; but now at Gilgal in Canaan, there was a memorable celebration of the feast. The recent Jordan crossing was similar to the crossing of the Red Sea. What vivid memories this brought to those who had come out of Egypt— for persons who were under 20 years of age at the Exodus were not excluded from Canaan. They remembered their fathers killing the lambs and sprinkling the blood on doorposts and lintels. They could still hear the awful death cry of the firstborn Egyptians. They recalled the excitement of the midnight departure, the terror of the Egyptian pursuit, and the thrill of passing between the walls of water to escape their Egyptian slave drivers.

As the lambs were slain for this first Passover near the Land of Promise, the Israelites were assured that just as the crossing of the Red Sea was followed by the destruction of the Egyptians, so would the passage of the Jordan be followed by the defeat of the Canaanites.

The Passover also pointed forward to the death of Christ, the Lamb of God. Paul wrote, "Christ our Passover also has been sacrificed" (1 Cor. 5:7), and as Christians we are commanded to remember that sacrifice by partaking of the Lord's Supper. But we do so with an eye on the future, for we celebrate His death in this manner only until He comes again. The Lord's Supper then is a connecting link between the past and the future, between the First and Second Advents of Christ, our Passover.

And for us too, the deliverance of the past sustains us in the present, and provides bright hope for tomorrow.

Dr. Hudson Armerding described an experience he had in Jerusalem.

After I checked into the hotel, an Arab assisted with my

suitcases. Not knowing whether the service was added to the bill, or whether the man should be paid on the spot, I said, "I am very sorry. I have just arrived in the country and I do not have change to give you." The man looked at me and with an expression I can still see said, "Sir, I don't need money; I need hope" (*Leadership*, Tyndale, p. 79).

The Appropriation of Canaan's Produce (5:11-12)

On the day after the Passover, the Israelites ate some of the produce of the land—unleavened cakes and parched corn. Since they gave evidence of wanting to be fully obedient to the Law of God, it is probable that they first brought the wave offering of a sheaf of grain as prescribed in Leviticus 23:10-14. Then the people ate freely of the harvest. Roasted ears of grain are still considered a delicacy in the Middle East, and are eaten as a substitute for bread.

God had promised to bring Israel into a land of abundance, "a land of wheat and barley, of vines and fig trees and pomegranates, a land of olive oil and honey; a land where you shall eat food without scarcity" (Deut. 8:8-9a). Now at last they had tasted the fruit of the land and realized it was only a foretaste of blessings to come.

The next day the manna ceased. For 40 long years it had continued, but now it stopped appearing as suddenly as it had begun, demonstrating that its provision was not a matter of chance but of special providence.

It is noteworthy that God did not discontinue the manna when Israel despised it (Num. 11:6), nor even when the unbelieving generation turned away from Kadesh-barnea and wandered in the trackless wilderness. He continued to give it for the sake of their children, who were now grown up and ready to enter the land of promise.

Can we expect God to work a miracle when natural means are available? There is no evidence that God works unnecessary miracles. We don't need food from heaven when we have bread from the earth.

The Acknowledgment of Their Divine Commander (5:13-15)

God had just brought the Israelites through three events: the rite of circumcision, the celebration of the Passover, and eating of Canaan's produce.

Now something happened which was for Joshua alone. It too was extremely meaningful and would soon be shared with the people.

It seemed obvious that the next step would be the capture of Jericho. But since no further message of instruction had come to Joshua, he went out to reconnoiter the seemingly impregnable fortress.

Joshua may have felt perplexed as he viewed the secure walls of Jericho. The spies reported at Kadesh-barnea that the cities of Canaan were "large and fortified to heaven" (Deut. 1:28). Despite Joshua's long military experience, he had never led an attack on a well-fortified city. Of the many fortresses in Palestine, Jericho was the most nearly invincible.

There was also the question of armaments. Israel's army had no siege engines, no battering rams, catapults, or moving towers. Their only weapons were slings, arrows, and spears—and these would be like straws against the fortified walls of Jericho.

Israel had no choice but to win the battle of Jericho. Now that they had crossed the Jordan, their troops had no place to which they could retreat. Furthermore, they could not bypass the city, because that would leave the women, children, goods, and cattle at Gilgal exposed to certain destruction.

Pondering such heavy thoughts, Joshua was startled to see a soldier brandishing his sword. Instinctively, he challenged the stranger: "Who goes there, friend or foe?" If he were a friend, an Israelite, he was off limits and had some serious explaining to do. And especially since Joshua had given no command for anyone to draw a sword! If the stranger were an enemy, Joshua was ready to fight!

"Are you for us, or for our adversaries?"

"No, rather I indeed come now as Captain of the host of the Lord."

Then something happened to convince Joshua that this was no mortal soldier. As with Abraham under the oak at Mamre, Jacob at Peniel, and Moses at the burning bush, there came a flash of revelation so that Joshua knew he was in the presence of God. It seems clear that Joshua was indeed talking to the Angel of Jehovah, in a theophanic Old Testament appearance of the Lord Jesus Christ Himself.

The Captain of the Lord's host stood with a drawn sword, indicating that He would fight with and for Israel. The sword also indicated that God's long-suffering delay of judgment was at an end. The iniquity of the Amorites was now intolerable and the Israelites were to be the instruments by whom judicial punishment would fall.

What kind of a military force did this divine Commander lead? The host of the Lord was surely not limited to the army of Israel. It may have referred to the host of heaven which surrounded Dothan, when Elisha and his servant appeared to be greatly outnumbered by the Syrian army (2 Kings 6:8-17). In the Garden of Gethsemane at the time of His arrest, Jesus spoke of the 12 legions of angels ready to defend Him (Matt. 26:53). In the Book of Hebrews, angels are described as "ministering spirits, sent out to render service for the sake of those who will inherit salvation" (1:14). Though invisible, they serve and care for us in times of great need. Only eternity will reveal the extent of their service and protection.

In June 1920, the people of Shansi, China were warned that bandits were coming. Villagers quickly made what preparation they could. One lone lady missionary within the village kept a mission school for about 40 girls. How was she to protect them from these lawless men? There were not enough soldiers in the village to offer effective resistance. She called all the girls together into the classroom, explained their danger, and calmly asked them all to kneel and commit themselves into the care of their almighty God.

"Oh, God, our heavenly Father," the missionary prayed, "we have no might but in Thee. Please send some guardian angels to protect us this night."

Hardly had the blanket of night fallen over the village when it seemed that all hell let loose its terrors. Wild shouts rent the air as armed men roamed the darkened streets at will. There were sounds of splintering wood as doors were broken in, and piteous cries for mercy from helpless men and women. Crackling fires started here and there, their lurid flames lighting up the black sky. Occasionally, a rifle shot punctuated the clamor with its message of death.

Toward morning all sounds died down to a whisper. The bandits had overrun the whole village, accomplishing their desires and then stealing away at dawn to their secret haunts in the hills. But not one of them had attempted to enter the mission school compound with the 40 girls sheltered within.

The missionary lady went out the next morning to offer what help she could in the village. The night's horrors were evident on every side. Some of the homes were gutted and still smoking from smoldering fires. Many doors were splintered or torn off their hinges. Dead bodies lay in the streets or astride open doorways. Young girls were weeping in the arms of their mothers. Other girls were absent, carried away by the bandits. Grief and despair marked all faces.

"God in His mercy spared us and our school of girls," said the missionary.

"No wonder!" the villagers replied with awe. "The bandits did not dare molest you. On the corners of your compound walls, standing on guard, we saw four angels with drawn swords in their hands!"

Recognizing his heavenly Visitor with drawn sword, Joshua fell on his face and worshiped, saying, "What has my Lord to say to His servant?"

The reply of the Lord to Joshua was brief but urgent: "Remove your sandals from your feet, for the place where you are standing is holy."

This was a deeply significant experience for Joshua. He was anticipating a battle between the Israelite and Canaanite armies. He had thought this was to be *his* war, until he confronted the divine Commander and learned that the battle was the Lord's. The Captain of the Lord's host had not come to be an idle spectator of the conflict; neither was He an ally. Rather, He was in complete charge and would shortly reveal His plans for the capture of the citadel of Jericho.

During World War I, when General Pershing placed the American army under the command of General Foch, commander of the Allied forces in the field, he said, "Infantry, artillery, aviation—all that we have is yours. Dispose of them as you will."

Though Joshua had little to offer the Captain of the Lord's host, he too said in effect, "All that we have is Yours. Use us as You will."

How comforting this must have been for Joshua. He did not need to bear alone the heavy burden of leadership. He gladly acknowledged that this battle and the entire conquest of Canaan was God's conflict, and that he was God's servant.

While Dr. C.I. Scofield was pastor of the First Congregational Church of Dallas, there came a time when the burdens of the ministry seemed heavier than he could bear. All but crushed by the weight of the frustrations and problems of the work, he knelt one day in his office. In deep agony of spirit, he opened the Scriptures, looking for some message of comfort and strength. Led by the Spirit to the closing verses of Joshua 5, he saw at once that he was trying to carry the responsibilities alone. That day he turned his ministry over to the Lord, assured that it was His work and that He would accomplish it. In accepting God's leadership, Dr. Scofield allied himself with God's power.

Are you aware of the unseen presence of our Captain, the Lord Jesus Christ? He will fight your battles for you if you will allow Him to do so. And such awareness will make a vast difference in the way you face life's problems!

5
Divine
Strategy for Victory

Joshua 6

> Joshua 'fit' the battle of Jericho,
> Jericho, Jericho,
> Joshua 'fit' the battle of Jericho,
> And the walls came a-tumblin' down!

So says the old spiritual. But if one thing is clear about the story of Jericho, it is that Joshua did not fight this battle at all.

The military strategy for the conquest of Canaan as a whole, and for Jericho in particular, was divinely provided. Furthermore, God was always present to give direction, and to fight Israel's battles.

The pattern of divine strategy was based on geographic factors. From their camp at Gilgal near the Jordan River, the Israelites could see steep hills to the west. Jericho controlled the way of ascent into these mountains. Ai, another fortress, stood at the head of the ascent. If the Israelites were to capture the hill country, they must certainly take Jericho and Ai. This would put them on top of the hill country and in control of the Central Ridge, having driven a wedge between the northern and southern sections of Canaan. Israel could then engage in battle the armies of the south without interference from the more remote enemy in the north.

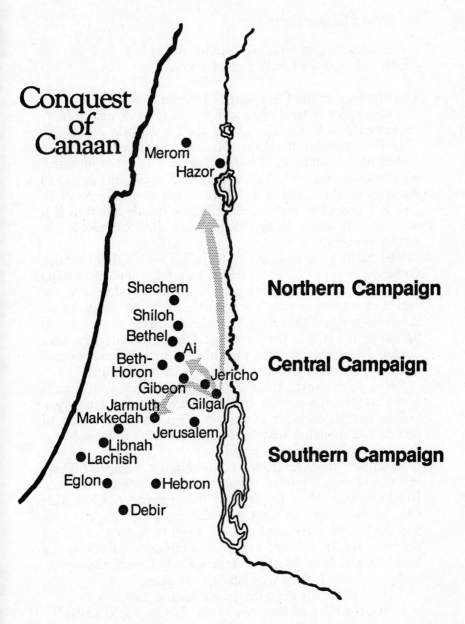

Conquest of Canaan

Merom

Hazor

Northern Campaign

Shechem

Shiloh

Bethel

Ai

Beth-Horon

Central Campaign

Jericho

Gibeon

Jarmuth

Gilgal

Makkedah

Jerusalem

Libnah

Southern Campaign

Lachish

Eglon

Hebron

Debir

But first, Jericho must fall—and it would if Joshua and the people followed the Lord's plan of action.

The Strategy of the Conquest of Jericho (6:1-7)

The impressive fortress of Jericho was in full view, as Joshua's conversation with the Captain of the Lord's host continued. This Commander, the Lord Himself, promised victory to Joshua and announced, "I have given Jericho into your hand, with its king, and the valiant warriors." The city, the king, and the army would all fall to Israel. The tense of the Hebrew verb *give* is a prophetic perfect, describing a future action as if it were already accomplished. Since God had declared it, the victory was assured.

The battle plan Joshua was to utilize was highly unusual. Ordinary weapons of war, such as battering rams and scaling ladders, were not to be employed. Rather, Joshua and the armed men were to march around the city once a day for six successive days, with seven priests blowing seven trumpets, and preceding the Ark of the Covenant. On the seventh day, after circling Jericho seven times, the walls of Jericho would collapse and the city would be taken "without a shot being fired."

Seven priests, seven trumpets, seven days, and seven circuits of the wall on the seventh day. The number *seven* often symbolizes completeness or perfection. This was God's plan of action; and though it may have seemed foolish to men, it was the perfect scheme for this battle.

What was the significance of the blaring trumpets? These instruments were jubilee trumpets used in connection with Israel's solemn feasts to proclaim the presence of God. This was not therefore a military undertaking, but a religious one, and the trumpets declared that the Lord of heaven and earth was weaving His invisible way around this doomed city. In the long blasts of these priestly trumpets, God Himself was saying,

Lift up your heads, O ye gates;
even lift them up, ye everlasting doors;
and the King of glory shall come in (Ps. 24:9, KJV).

No battle strategy could have appeared more unreasonable than this one. What was to prevent the army of Jericho from raining arrows and spears down upon the defenseless Israelites? Or who could stop the enemy from rushing out of the several city gates to break up Israel's line, separating and then slaughtering them?

Joshua was an experienced military leader. Certainly these and similar objections to the divine strategy flashed into his mind. But unlike Moses, who had argued with lengthy eloquence against Jehovah's plan, Joshua responded with an unquestioning obedience. He lost no time in calling together the priests and leaders of the people, passing on to them the directions he had received from his Commander-in-Chief.

Dawson Trotman, founder of The Navigators, had a military background. On occasion he would line up his children and beginning with the oldest would ask, "What do your mother and I ask you to do?"

The child would reply, "One thing, Sir!"

Trotman would proceed down the row asking the same question of each child. Returning to the oldest he would question, "And what is that one thing?"

"To do everything you say, Sir!"

Faith expressed in obedience to God's Word is always the key to victory.

Most Christians have armed cities to conquer after they enter Canaan, and many have one particularly difficult conquest to make—one special "Jericho" that stands menacingly across the path of their spiritual progress. In some cases it may be a dispositional weakness—indifference, materialism, indolence, lust. In other cases it may be a difficult domestic or work situation, or a perplexing financial problem (*Bible Knowledge,* Scripture Press, April 1963, p. 53).

We too must learn that victory over our "Jerichos" will come only as we learn to trust and obey. We may not understand God's method and plans, but if we want to overcome our temptations and obstacles, we must submit to His way. The Apostle Paul wrote, "The weapons of our warfare are not of the flesh, but divinely powerful for the destruction of fortresses" (2 Cor. 10:4).

The Sequence of the Conquest of Jericho (6:8-21)

Shortly after dawn, a long procession began to wind out of the camp of Israel. First came the armed men, marching under tribal banners; then seven priests with trumpets; next the ark of God, and lastly the rear guard. Although the army was prominent in the procession, Jericho would not fall through its prowess, but by the power of God.

In silence, the procession made its way toward Jericho, once a day for six days, winding around the city as a serpent. Jericho covered about nine acres; the march around took 25 to 35 minutes. When the silent circuit was completed, the Israelites would quietly return to camp.

We are compelled to ask, "Why this seemingly irrational strategy?" No other fortress had ever been conquered in such fashion.

• The strategy was to test the faith of Joshua. He did not question; he trusted and obeyed.

• It was also designed to test Israel's obedience to the will of God. And that was not easy in this situation; for they were exposing themselves every day to ridicule and danger.

It appears that the Israelites were given orders on a daily basis, so that their obedience was not a once-for-all matter, but a new challenge every morning. That is the way God generally deals with us too. We live today with little or no knowledge of tomorrow.

He does not open His whole hand at once, He opens a finger at a time, as you do sometimes with your children when you are trying to coax them to take something out of the palm. He gives us enough light for the moment. He says, "March around Jericho; and be sure that I mean something. What I do mean I will tell you someday."

And so we have to put all into His hands" (Alexander Maclaren, *Expositions of Holy Scripture,* III, p. 136).

The faith of the sons of Israel triumphed over fear that the enemy would attack as well as over the expectation of ridicule and scorn. Never before and seldom after this historic event did the thermometer of faith rise so high in Israel.

• Finally, this plan was designed to strike fear into the hearts of the inhabitants of Jericho. It succeeded here as well. As the Israelites continued their solemn, daily march, ridicule faded from the enemies' lips as they asked, "What new type of strategy is this? . . . When and how will they attack?"

When General Montgomery took command in North Africa in World War II, he uncovered the cause for military losses the Allied forces had been suffering: "Previously, orders had generally been queried by subordinates right down the line. I was determined to stop this state of affairs at once." Under Montgomery, orders no longer formed the basis for discussion. He expected action.

Joshua and the soldiers of Israel were to win an important victory because they received and obeyed their orders, without questioning or revising them.

On that fateful seventh day, the procession made the circuit of the walls seven times. At the end of the seventh circuit, the clear voice of Joshua rang out, "Shout, for the Lord has given you the city." So when the priests gave a blast on the trumpets, the people "shouted with a great shout." And what a shout that was, as the Israelites gave release to their repressed emotions and stifled voices. It was a shout that reverberated through the hills around, startling the wild creatures in their dens and terrorizing the dwellers of Jericho in their homes. At that moment when the air was rent, the wall of Jericho, obeying the summons of God, toppled into ruin.

The men of Israel clambered over the debris. Finding the inhabitants paralyzed with terror and unable to resist, they utterly destroyed all human and animal life in Jericho, except Rahab and her household.

It is strikingly clear from the context that Israel was acting on divine command. The ultimate responsibility for the slaughter rested therefore with God and not the Israelites. Jericho was placed under the ban, which meant that Jericho and all its contents would be devoted to Jehovah as the firstfruits of the land. This signified that Israel would receive all of Canaan from Him. No booty was to be taken by the people. In the execution of the ban, men and animals were to be killed; objects would either be destroyed, or set apart for the purposes of the sanctuary.

It is important to remember that God has the right to visit judgment on individuals and nations. The idolatrous worship and licentious lifestyle, so clearly attested by archeological discoveries (such as the Ras Shamra Tablets) gave cause for the divine judgment on Jericho.

God's purpose was to bless the nation of Israel in the land and to use her as a means of blessing the world. But this blessing would be greatly hindered if Israel were infected by the degenerate religion of the Canaanites. Gleason Archer pointedly declares,

In view of the corrupting influence of the Canaanite religion, especially with its religious prostitution . . . and infant sacrifice, it was impossible for pure faith and worship to be maintained in Israel except by the complete elimination of the Canaanites themselves (*A Survey of Old Testament Introduction,* Moody Press, p. 261).

Sin is desperately contagious. To compromise with evil in our lives is dangerous, and invites spiritual disaster.

Charles Haddon Spurgeon told of a lady who advertised for a chauffeur. Three men applied and were asked one question: "How close could you drive to the edge of a precipice without losing control?"

One answered, "Within six inches."

The next said, "To within a hairbreadth of the edge."

The third one replied, "Lady, if you want a daredevil for a driver, I am not your man. My policy has always been to keep as far away from danger as possible." The third man was immediately hired. Just so, flirting with sin is dangerous. This is why God commanded the destruction of Jericho and why He expects Christians today to judge sin in their lives.

One question asks for an answer: Why did the walls of Jericho fall right at the moment when the people shouted? Did an earthquake occur and cause the destruction? Were Israelite soldiers undermining the walls while the others marched? Did vibrations set up by the trumpet blasts and soldiers' shouts bring the collapse? Were shock waves, caused by the marching feet of the Israelites, responsible? The narrative leaves little or no room for such speculation. That it was a supernatural event is clear from the fact that the walls were completely destroyed, except the portion surrounding the house of Rahab. Must we know the means God employs in a miracle? A New Testament writer, reviewing the event centuries later, was content to write, "By faith the walls of Jericho fell down, after they had been encircled for seven days" (Heb. 11:30).

Archeological evidence for the collapse of Jericho's walls in Joshua's day is not as clear as was once supposed. Further excavations have determined that in its long history, Jericho has had 34 walls. It is estimated that the area suffered about four earthquakes a century. The thoroughness of Joshua's destruction of the city, and the process of erosion over five centuries until it was refortified in Ahab's time, also contribute to the meager remains and the extreme difficulty of relating these remains to the time of Joshua's attack.

The most significant evidence seems to be the extensive pottery remains found on the mound and in the tombs of the area, pointing to occupancy of Jericho until about 1,400 B.C. Under the pottery is a thick burned layer of ash representing a major destruction to be identified with that of Joshua who had destroyed and burned the city. (For an excellent discussion of the archeology of Old Testament Jericho, see Leon Wood, *A Survey of Israel's History*, Zondervan, pp. 94-99).

The Sequel to the Conquest of Jericho (6:22-27)

Joshua kept the promise made to Rahab by the two spies, and sent those young men to the house where the scarlet cord hung from the window. She must have greeted them joyfully, following them without hesitation to the appointed place outside the doomed city. Rahab and her family were Gentiles and in need of ceremonial cleansing. The men had to be circumcised before they could be identified with the people of Israel.

Rahab's history is a remarkable example of the grace of God operating in the life of an individual and a family. Regardless of her past life, she was saved by faith in the living God and even became a part of the messianic line (Matt. 1:5). In addition, in keeping with the biblical pattern, when divine judgment descended, she and her family were spared. The same was true for Noah and his family, and Lot and his family. And believers today can likewise rejoice in the fact that when God is ready to pour out the judgments of the Tribulation on this earth, He will first deliver His own to a place of safety. Paul affirmed, "For God has not destined us for wrath, but for obtaining salvation through our Lord Jesus Christ" (1 Thes. 5:9).

The story of Rahab also shows how great a blessing a woman can be to her family.

Men, as heads of households, are responsible for a family's spiritual welfare, but women have been committed a share in that responsibility and frequently discharge it more faithfully than their husbands. Timothy's mother and grandmother may have had more influence on him than his father. Monica, mother of Augustine, wrestled in prayer in behalf of her wayward son and gave the world one of Christendom's great theologians. Wives, mothers, sisters, aunts, and grandmothers—all may exert great influence, through godly living and faithful prayer, on husbands, sons, brothers, nephews, and grandsons (*Bible Knowledge*, March 1972, p. 45).

Jericho's placement under the ban included the pronouncement of a curse on anyone who would dare to refortify the city by rebuilding a wall around it. Though the site was apparently occupied for brief periods, the anathema was not violated until the days of King Ahab, 500 years later. As a sign of the apostasy of that period, Hiel the Bethelite attempted to rebuild Jericho's walls. This cost the lives of his two sons (1 Kings 16:34).

The secret to success at Jericho was not Joshua's military genius or the army's skill in warfare. Victory came because the leaders and the people fully trusted God and obeyed His commands. "So the Lord was with Joshua, and his fame was in all the land."

This is what walking by faith is all about—in any generation. We all face "Jerichos" at one time or another, and we too can see the walls crumble as we trust God for victory.

Walking by Faith

But what does it mean to walk by faith? How does one walk this way? Pastor Richard Halverson has answered this question:

Walking by faith means walking not by sight. Does this mean that one walks blindly?

No more than the pilot of a 747 flies blind when he is being talked into a landing by the control tower.

No more than when a pilot believes his instruments rather than the seat of his pants.

One of the hard lessons a pilot learns is to trust his instruments when they disagree with his feel.

He is in much greater danger by depending on his feeling than by depending upon his instruments.

Ceiling zero—visibility zero—very poor conditions to fly by sight . . .

But the aircraft lands safely when the pilot listens to the word from the control tower and obeys it.

To walk by faith is to heed the Word of God . . . to read it, to know it, to learn it, to obey it.

It isn't those who walk by faith that louse up their lives. . . . Rather, it is those who walk by sight!

Jesus said, "I am the Light of the world, he who follows Me shall not walk in the darkness, but shall have the Light of life"—John 8:12 (*Perspective*, May 10, 1978).

6
The Agony
of Defeat

Joshua 7-8

Lake Placid, New York, a Christmas card village hidden among the aspen and white slopes of the Adirondacks, was host to the 1980 Winter Olympics. The crowds that came to watch the spectacular events, and the millions more who viewed by television, thrilled to feats of the skiers, bobsledders, and skaters. For many performers, there was the thrill of victory. But others felt the agony of defeat.

Unexpectedly, Israel tasted defeat. Up to this point in the conquest, the armies led by Joshua had experienced only victory. The possibility of a military defeat was the remotest thing from their minds, particularly since the smashing triumph over Jericho. Yet God's people are never more vulnerable, never in greater danger, than right after they have won a great victory.

Ai was the next on Israel's path of conquest. It was a smaller fortress than Jericho but in a strategic location on the eastern edge of the country's central ridge. The defeat of Ai would mean that the Israelites would hold the hill country, as well as commanding the route from Gilgal into the interior.

Archelogists have often identified Ai with the site of et-Tell. But excavations show that this location was not occupied from

2,400-1,200 B.C. It was therefore already in ruins when Joshua invaded in 1,400 B.C. The exact location of Ai is yet to be determined. Though we are not able to sift the ruins of Ai, we can observe the importance of the happenings there from the amount of biblical material given to a discussion of Israel's defeat, as well as of her victory at that location.

Defeat at Ai (7:1-26)

Jericho had been placed under the ban, meaning that everything living was to be put to death, and that valuable objects were to be dedicated to the Lord's treasury. No Israelite soldier was to help himself to the booty. But that very temptation was too strong for one man, Achan.

1. Disobedience (v. 1). Alexander Whyte has drawn an imaginative picture of Achan's downfall:

Who is that stealing about among the smoking ruins? Is that some soldier of Jericho who has saved himself from the devouring sword? When the night wind wakens the embers again, these are the accoutrements and movements of one of Joshua's men. Has he lost his way? Has he been half dead, and has he not heard the rally of the trumpet? He hides, he listens, he looks through the darkness, he disappears into the darkness (*Bible Characters,* First Series, Zondervan, p. 292).

Though we might wish to applaud the discipline of Joshua's forces—only one of his soldiers gave way in the time of temptation—yet even one did not escape God's notice. Sin never escapes the watchful eye of God.

A seminary professor was counseling with a couple who were having severe marital problems. After some discussion the husband said, "We certainly don't want the Lord to know about this."

Not only did God see Achan's sin; because of it His wrath burned against the entire nation. He considered the people collectively responsible and withheld His blessing until the matter was made right. In fact it seems apparent that Israel's history would have ended there if God had not turned away from His anger.

2. Defeat (vv. 2-5). Unaware of Achan's disobedience and eager to take advantage of the first victory, Joshua made preparations for the next battle by sending spies 10 miles northwest to Ai.

When the spies returned they spoke with great confidence: "If you think Jericho fell with ease, wait until we get to Ai. We can conquer them easily with two or three thousand men!"

But the spies were wrong. When God gave the orders to Joshua, He told him to take "all the people of war" (8:1). Though not as large as Jericho, Ai was well-fortified and her soliders well-entrenched. Israel was guilty of underestimating the strength of her enemy and of overestimating her own strength. On this occasion, there is no mention of prayer and no evidence of dependence on God.

It is a deadly error to underrate the enemy's power. Christians are often guilty of this and suffer the consequences in ignominious spiritual defeat.

The calamity which befell Israel was due, at least in part, to minimizing the enemy and to assuming that one victory guaranteed another. But it simply doesn't work that way. Yesterday's victory does not make us immune from defeat today. There must be a continuing dependence on the Lord for strength. In the context of the Christian's conflict with evil, Paul wrote, "Be strong in the Lord, and in the strength of His might" (Eph. 6:10).

Instead of sending his entire army, Joshua sent only 3,000 men to Ai. Instead of conquering, his army was routed, and they fled,

> rushing in wild terror down the steep pass which they had so confidently breasted in the morning, till the pursuers caught them up at some "quarries," where, perhaps, the ground was difficult, and there slew the few who fell, while the remainder got away by swiftness of foot, and brought back their terror and shame to the camp

(A. Maclaren, *Expositions of Holy Scripture*, III, p. 147).

And as the report of the defeat spread rapidly through the camp, the people were utterly demoralized. "The hearts of the people melted and became as water." The most significant matter here was not the defeat itself, nor even the 36 slain soldiers. It was that Israel was suddenly filled with terrible misgivings. Jehovah's help had been withdrawn, seemingly without reason. Had God changed His mind?

3. Dismay (vv. 6-9). Joshua too was stunned by the defeat. In keeping with ancient rites of mourning, he and the elders tore their clothes, put dust on their heads, and fell on their faces before the ark of the Lord until evening. Then Joshua verbalized his perplexity in three questions:

• "Why did You ever bring this people across the Jordan, to deliver us into the hands of the Amorites to destroy us? If only we had been content to stay on the other side of the Jordan!"

• "What can I say, now that Israel has been routed by its enemies? The Canaanites . . . will hear about this and they will surround us and wipe out our name from the earth."

• "What then will You do for Your own great name?" (vv. 7-9, NIV).

At first it appeared that Joshua was blaming God for the defeat and not even considering that the cause might lie in another quarter. He even adopted the thinking of the spies against whom he had so vehemently protested at Kadesh-barnea. They had said, "Would that we had died in the land of Egypt! Or would that we had died in this wilderness! And why is the Lord bringing us into this land, to fall by the sword? Our wives and our little ones will become plunder (Num. 14:2-3).

Joshua's greatest concern was that the news of this defeat might somehow reduce heathen respect for God's own name.

Joshua's reactions reveal how very human he was, and it is at this point that we feel a kinship with him. For in the dark moments of discouragement and defeat, every one of us has forgotten the promises of God and the previous victories. Sadly, it is all too easy to forget in the dark what God has revealed to us in the light.

4. *Directions (vv. 10-15).* The Lord's reply to Joshua was brusque: "Rise up! Why is it that you have fallen on your face?" He proceeded to explain the cause of the defeat and the need for action. The cause of the disaster was with Israel, not with God—Israel had sinned. Then God delivered the indictment by means of an "indignant accumulation of verbs" (Maclaren). Advancing from the general to the particular, Israel was charged with sinning, breaching the covenant, appropriating things under the ban, stealing, deceiving, and concealing the stolen goods. And until these transgressions were repudiated and expiation made for them, the sin of Achan would be considered the sin of the nation.

In effect, God said, "Joshua, do you not remember what caused the defeat of Israel at Kadesh and their subsequent wanderings for 38 years in the wilderness? Sin has once again come among My people, and that is why you should not be here on your face. This is not a time for prayer but for action. The sin in the camp must be dealt with!"

After the fall of Jericho it was recorded, "So the Lord was with Joshua" (6:27). But now the grim announcement came from God: He would not be with Joshua unless the sin was judged.

Sin causes the loss of God's presence and power. Sin shuts off the showers of God's blessing. Sin stifles and strangles the abundant life promised in Jesus Christ. Sin paralyzes and immobilizes the life of the individual believer and of the local body. God's message to Joshua applies also to God's people today in times of obvious spiritual defeat and decline; namely, deal with sin! (Wesley G. Hunt, "Sin in the Camp," *The Sunday School Times and Gospel Herald*, November 15, 1973, p. 13).

Many years ago, as the student pastor of a small church, I was baffled by the lack of visible growth and the seeming absence of God's blessing. One Sunday a young woman offered her resignation as a Sunday School teacher, explaining that she too was concerned about the condition of the church. She confessed that she felt she was the "Achan in the camp."

We do not part with sin easily. Augustine, in a revealing passage of his *Confessions*, admitted that as a young man he often prayed, "O God, give me chastity, but not yet."

Imagine Jesus coming to a woman possessed with seven demons. He says to her, "Woman, do you want me to cast out your demons and set you completely free?"

The woman answered, "Yes, Lord. But may I ask a favor? Will You cast out only six?"

In the case of Achan, there could be no temporizing. Judgment had to be decisive and complete. The Lord proceeded to reveal the steps in the purging process. First, the people were to sanctify themselves. On the next day they were to gather for the identification of the offender, presumably by the casting of lots. The culprit was then to be destroyed, because he had "committed a disgraceful thing in Israel."

5. Discovery (vv. 16-21). Joshua rose early on the fateful day. All Israel was assembled for the sacred ritual of drawing lots. The method probably called for the selecting of inscribed potsherds out of a jar. Since God knew who was guilty, why didn't He simply reveal the identity to Joshua? Most certainly this dramatic method would impress upon the nation of Israel the seriousness of disobeying God's commands. It would also give the guilty person an opportunity to repent of his sin. If Achan had responded in this way, throwing himself on the mercy of God, he would no doubt have been pardoned, as the guilty David was centuries later.

There was a grim silence as the casting of lots selected the tribe of Judah, the family of the Zerhrites, the household of Zabdi, and finally the trespasser himself, Achan. This was no quirk of fate but the direction of God's providence.

Solomon described the process well, "The lot is cast into the lap; but its every decision is from the Lord" (Prov. 16:33).

Strangely, Achan remained silent throughout the entire procedure. Surely fear must have gripped him, and his heart pounded furiously as each step brought his discovery nearer.

At length Joshua addressed Achan, tenderly but firmly. Although he hated the sin, he did not despise the sinner. A public confession was necessary to confirm the supernatural exposure of the guilty person.

Achan's response was straightforward and complete. He confessed his sin and gave no excuses. But neither did he express sorrow for having disobeyed God's Word, for having betrayed his nation for booty, for having caused the defeat of Israel's army and the death of 36 men.

The three crucial steps of Achan's sin are familiar ones: he saw; he coveted; he took. Eve followed the same tragic steps in the Garden of Eden (Gen. 3:6), and so did David with Bathsheba (2 Sam. 11:2-4).

The material objects Achan hid under the floor of his tent included a beautiful mantle of Shinar, an ingot of gold, and some lumps or rings of silver. Achan may well have reasoned, "After all, I have been deprived of the good things of life these many years in the wilderness. Here is a beautiful new and stylish garment and some gold and silver. Why would God want to withhold these things from me? They will never be missed—and I am entitled to some pleasure and prosperity!"

But there was a specific command against touching any of Jericho's booty for personal use. God's Word can never be rationalized away without penalty.

Basically, Achan was caught in the web of materialism, a problem that also faces us in this century. It has been estimated that Americans are bombarded by 1,700 advertisements a day via various forms of the media. While there is no danger of our purchasing all 1,700 items, there is the possibility of our accepting the philosophy behind those advertisements—that we will have complete, fulfilled, satisfied lives if only we drive this car, use this hair spray, or drink that beverage.

The Christian should take a long look at the covetous Achan

and then remember Paul's exhortation to put to death covetousness, "which amounts to idolatry" (Col. 3:5b). Satan tempts us to compromise and sin through our inordinate desire for material things. Jesus said, "Beware, and be on your guard against every form of greed; for not even when one has an abundance does his life consist of his possessions" (Luke 12:15).

6. *Death (vv. 22-26)*. Achan's confession was quickly verified as the stolen objects were laid out before the Lord. Then the wretched man was led out to the Valley of Achor, along with all his household. The fatal stones fell on Achan and his children, fire consuming their bodies and belongings. Having stolen devoted objects, Achan himself became contaminated. In view of the fact that the Law prohibits the execution of children for their father's sins (Deut. 24:16), we assume that Achan's children were accomplices in crime.

A marker in the form of a great heap of stones was raised over the body of Achan. This seems to have been a common method of burial for infamous individuals, and served in this case the good purpose of warning Israel against the sin of disobeying God's express commands.

Thus Achan, whose name meant "troubler," was buried in the Valley of Achor, or the Valley of Troubling. And because Israel was willing to deal with the sin problem, God's burning anger was turned away and He was ready to lead them again to victory.

There once existed in Russia a noble order of merit, which was much coveted by the princes and nobles. It was conferred by the czar only on his favorites or on distinguished heroes of the kingdom. But another group shared its honor in a very dubious form. Those nobles who became a burden to the czar, or stood in his way, received the decoration only to die. The pin point was tipped with poison, and when the decoration was being fastened on the chest by the imperial messenger, the flesh of the person was accidentally pricked. Next morning the individual who had received the coveted honor was dead.

The very things Achan coveted brought his death. This chapter is an awesome reminder that the "wages of sin is death" (Rom. 6:23), and that "when lust has conceived, it gives birth to sin; and when sin is accomplished, it brings forth death" (James 1:15).

Victory at Ai (8:1-35)

During the heady days of World War I, Kaiser Wilhelm and his generals adopted the motto, "GOTT MIT UNS" or "God with us."

The northern preachers who visited President Lincoln, when the American Civil War hung in the balance, also affirmed that God was on their side. But Lincoln replied quickly, "No, friends, rather pray that we may be found on God's side."

After the defeat at Ai, Joshua might well have wondered if Israel were on God's side.

But with Achan's crime judged, God's favor toward Israel was restored, and He reassured Joshua that He had not forsaken him or the people. Then the Lord said to Joshua, "Do not fear or be dismayed."

When Joshua heard these words, his heart quickened, for these were the same words Moses had spoken in Kadesh-barnea as he sent out the 12 spies (Deut. 1:21). They were also the words Moses had said to Joshua 40 years later as he turned the reins of leadership over to the younger man (Deut. 31:8). Joshua heard them again from God, just after the death of Moses (Josh. 1:9).

Now at this crucial time in Joshua's life, it was good to be reminded and reassured that God was ready to lead, if Joshua was ready to listen to *His* plan.

1. The setting of the battle (vv. 1-2). God's plan involved using all the fighting men of Israel. While the primary cause of the defeat at Ai was Achan's sin, the secondary cause was the underrating of the enemy.

The divine plan also included returning to Ai, the place of Israel's humiliating defeat. God said, "Arise, go up to Ai."

And He promised to turn the place of defeat into a place of victory.

Historians tell us of an Italian naval engagement that took place in the 16th century, between the fleets of Genoa and Venice. The Genoese admiral sustained a crushing defeat; but after repairs to his ships were completed, he ordered his men to set sail for the scene of the former battle.

"What?" asked the officers. "Return to the place where we were routed?"

"Yes," replied the admiral. "It was rendered famous by our defeat, and I will make it immortal by our victory!"

When our fellowship with God is broken by sin, restoration is possible only as we identify the sin, confessing it to God and claiming His forgiveness (1 John 1:9). Only in this way can our defeats be turned into victories.

Before the actual plan of battle was revealed to Joshua, he was told that the spoil of Ai could be taken by Israel. Jericho had been placed under the ban, but Ai was not.

What an irony! If only Achan had suppressed his greedy and selfish desires and obeyed God's word at Jericho, he would later have had all that his heart desired—and God's blessing too. How easy it is to take matters into our own hands and go ahead of the Lord!

2. *The sequence of the battle (vv. 3-29).* The order of events at Ai was entirely different than at Jericho. The Israelites did not march around the walls of Ai seven times, nor did the walls fall miraculously. Israel had to conquer the city through the normal operations of war. God is not limited to any one method of working. He is not stereotyped in His operations.

We Christians should not be surprised when the Holy Spirit leads us in different ways at different times. He will not contradict His own principles or character as set forth in the Scriptures, but He will not act like a machine, always responding to similar situations in exactly the same ways. When a Christian falls into the idea that because

Jericho has been taken one way Ai must be taken the same way, he has stopped thinking of God as personal (Francis Schaeffer, *Joshua and the Flow of Biblical History*, InterVarsity Press, pp. 112-13).

The strategy for the capture of Ai was ingenious. God told Joshua to place an ambush behind the city. The outworking of this plan involved three contingents of soldiers.

• The first was a group of valiant warriors who were sent by night to hide just west of the city of Ai. Their assignment was to rush into the city and burn it after its defenders had deserted it to pursue Joshua and his army. While the text indicates this unit numbered 30,000, this seems an excessively large number of men to hide near the city. Since the Hebrew word translated "thousand" may also be rendered "chief" or "officer," it appears better to view this as a choice group of 30 brave officers chosen by Joshua for a daring commando-type mission.

• The second contingent was the main army which came the 15 miles from Gilgal early the next morning and camped in plain view on the north side of Ai. Led by Joshua, this army was a diversionary force to decoy the defenders of Ai out of the city.

• The third contingent was another ambush unit of 5,000 men who were positioned between Bethel and Ai to cut off the possibility of reinforcements from Bethel to aid the men of Ai.

The plan worked to perfection. When the king of Ai saw Israel's army, he took the bait. Pursuing the Israelites who pretended defeat, the men of Ai left their city unguarded. At Joshua's signal, the commando troops quickly entered and set the city on fire. The consternation of the men of Ai was complete as they witnessed the billows of flame and smoke rising into the sky. But before they could gather their wits, they were caught in a pincerlike movement of Israelite soldiers.

Reentering the city, Israel's army brought death to all Ai's inhabitants, and Joshua burned the city to the ground. Ai's king, previously spared, was now hung and buried beneath a pile of stones.

Thus Israel, restored to God's favor, won a great victory. After failure there was a second chance. We too should remember that one defeat or failure does not signal the end of usefulness for God. He is ready to forgive us, restore us, and use us.

3. The sequel to the battle (vv. 30-35). Following the victory at Ai, Joshua did something that seemed militarily foolish. Instead of securing the central sector of the land with further victories, he led the Israelites on a spiritual pilgrimage that Moses had earlier commanded (Deut. 27).

Without delay Joshua led the men, women, children, and cattle from Gilgal northward up the Jordan Valley to the place specified, the mountains of Ebal and Gerizim which were at Shechem. The march of about 30 miles was not difficult or dangerous, since they passed through a very sparsely populated area. But how did the Israelites avoid a confrontation with the men of the city of Shechem? For this fortress guarded the entrance to the valley between the mountains.

Of course the Bible does not record every battle of the conquest and the record of the capture of Shechem may have been omitted. On the other hand, the city may at this time have been in friendly hands or it may simply have surrendered without resistance. But why was this location chosen? Because these mountains are located in the geographic center of the land and from either peak a great deal of the Promised Land can be seen.

Here then, in a place that represented all of the land, both at the time of entrance into Canaan—and later when his leadership was ending (Josh. 24:1)—Joshua challenged the people to renew their covenant vows to Jehovah. The solemn and significant religious ceremonies at this location involved three things.

• An altar of stones was erected on Mt. Ebal and sacrifices were offered to the Lord. Jericho and Ai, in which the false gods of the Canaanites were worshiped, had fallen. Israel publicly worshiped and proclaimed faith in the one true God.

• Joshua set up some large stone pillars and on their whitewashed surfaces wrote, "a copy of the Law of Moses." Just how much of the Law was inscribed cannot be determined. Some suggest only the Ten Commandments while others feel it included Deuteronomy 5—26. Archeologists have discovered similarly inscribed pillars or stelae from six to eight feet in height, in other Middle East locations. The Behistun inscription in Iran is three times the length of the Book of Deuteronomy!

• The Law was read to the people. Half the people were positioned on the slopes of Mt. Gerizim to the south; the other half were on the slopes of Mt. Ebal to the north; and the Ark of the Covenant surrounded by priests was in the valley between. The large natural amphitheater made it possible for the people to hear every word.

As the curses of the Law were read one by one, the tribes on Mt. Ebal responded, "Amen!" As the blessings were read, the tribes on Mt. Gerizim responded, "Amen!" (See Deut. 27:12-26.) With all sincerity Israel affirmed that the Law of the Lord was indeed to be the law of the land.

God was giving the people a huge object lesson; what happened to them in the land was going to depend, as it were, on whether they were living on Mt. Gerizim or Mt. Ebal. The people were to hear from Mt. Gerizim the blessings which would come to them if they kept God's Law and from Mt. Ebal the curses which would fall upon them, if they did not (Schaeffer, *Joshua and the Flow*, p. 121).

The history of the Jewish people since that time has been determined by their attitude toward the Law. When they have been obedient, they have experienced the blessing of God. And when they have been disobedient, judgment (Deut. 28). What tragedy that the affirmations of this momentous hour faded so quickly!

But has our nation done any better? Is the Law of the Lord the law of our land? Admittedly, our pluralistic society is not bound to God in a covenant relationship as ancient Israel was, but God's moral precepts from both Old and New Testaments furnish irreplaceable guidelines for building successful lives, whether national or individual.

The wise man of Old Testament times wrote, "Righteousness exalts a nation, but sin is a disgrace to any people" (Prov. 14:34).

Woodrow Wilson in his last public address said, "The sum of the whole matter is this, that our civilization cannot survive materially unless it is redeemed spiritually."

The survival of the United States may well depend on the willingness of all the people, leaders in Washington and citizens across the land, to allow the absolutes of God's Word to become the law of the land. And Christians must lead the way.

7
The Peril
of Prayerlessness

Joshua 9-10

As he knelt at Valley Forge, George Washington was keenly aware that unless God aided his bedraggled and discouraged army, all was lost.

During the Civil War, Abraham Lincoln confessed to a friend that he was often driven to his knees to pray because he had nowhere else to go.

Of a veteran missionary it was said, that "throughout his life his first step was always to pray; it was never his last resort."

Israel's failure to consult the Lord was a major factor in her defeat at Ai, and the prayerlessness of her leaders was about to precipitate another crisis.

The people had just returned to camp at Gilgal after hearing the Word of God read to them from Mt. Ebal and Mt. Gerizim. They had affirmed their willingness to obey the Word of God. Because it was a time of spiritual victory; it was also a time for a subtle attack from Satan. When God's people think they have it made, they are most vulnerable to the enemy's assault.

The Alliance with the Gibeonites (9:1-27)

Israel's victories over Jericho and Ai roused surrounding nations to concerted action. The frightened kings grouped in three geographical areas: the hill country of central Palestine, the valleys or lowlands, and the coastal plain stretching north to Lebanon. That they were not able to unite as planned into one fighting force is a tribute to the success of Joshua's strategy to drive a wedge through the backbone of Canaan.

But powerful confederations did form in both the north and the south. Truces were declared in tribal wars, as deadly enemies prepared to make common cause against the invasion force of God's people.

When righteousness becomes aggressive, it has a way of uniting the forces of good—and also of evil. It happened this way when Jesus Christ walked this earth. His fearless proclamation of truth and exposure of evil united Pharisees, Sadducees, and Herodians against Him. And when He returns, it will be the same. (See Ps. 2:2; Rev. 19:19.)

The more the Christian faith advances, the more vocal and violent the opposition will become. Recent reports indicate that Soviet leaders, alarmed over the religious interest of many young people, plan to intensify efforts to teach atheism. Exiled Soviet pastor Georgi Vins, who spent eight years in Russian labor camps, has described how evangelicals in that land are increasingly the target of repressive measures.

1. Deception of the Gibeonites (vv. 3-15). But not all of Israel's enemies wanted to fight. The Gibeonites were convinced they could never defeat Israel in war; therefore, they pursued peace. Located in the hill country only six miles northwest of Jerusalem, Gibeon was the head of a small confederate republic including three neighboring towns.

After consultation, the Gibeonites adopted an ingenious plan to send emissaries to Joshua, disguised as weary and worn travelers who had been on a long journey. When this strange deputation arrived in Gilgal, their garments were dirty and torn, their food was dry and moldy, their wineskins old and patched, and their sandals worn thin. The visitors declared to Joshua, "We have come from a far country; now therefore, make a covenant with us."

Why their emphasis on being from a far country and their deceptive performance to prove it? Apparently, the Gibeonites were aware of the provisions in the Mosaic Law permitting Israel to make peace with distant cities but requiring them to wipe out the cities of the nearby Canaanite nations (Deut. 20:10-15).

At first Joshua and his staff were hesitant: "Perhaps you are living within our land; how then shall we make a covenant with you?" It was well for them to be on their guard, for things are not always as they seem. Evil men are known to take advantage of the righteous. We too must always be on the alert, lest we fall prey to wolves masquerading in sheep's clothing. Jesus warned His disciples, "Behold, I send you out as sheep in the midst of wolves; therefore be shrewd as serpents, and innocent as doves" (Matt. 10:16).

As Joshua questioned them, the wily Gibeonites told their tale. They insisted they came from a great distance to show respect to the powerful God of the Israelites, and to be allowed to live at peace as Israel's servants. Interestingly, they made no mention of Israel's recent victories over Jericho and Ai; people from a far country would not have heard of these recent battles. Then they presented their credentials—the moldy bread, patched wineskins, ragged clothes—and the suspicion of Joshua and the leaders dissipated.

Caught off guard by the cunning strategy of the Gibeonites, the leaders of Israel concluded a formal treaty with them.

But Joshua and the Israelites made at least two mistakes. In the first place they accepted for evidence things that were highly questionable. Envoys with power to conclude a treaty with another nation should have had substantial credentials. It was foolish of Joshua not to demand them.

Many today are equally as gullible, accepting dubious declarations as scientific fact. Dr. Carl Armerding declared, "When we hear some supposedly learned man talk about the skeletal remains of prehistoric man whose age runs into hundreds of thousands of years, one wonders if this is not some more of the devil's moldy bread" (*The Fight for Palestine*, Van Kampen Press, pp. 91-92).

Yet what Christian is there who has not been similarly tempted by Satan, who has not been offered some of his "moldy bread"? Paul exhorted believers, "Put on the full armor of God, that you may be able to stand firm against the schemes of the devil" (Eph. 6:11). We need to know that the enemy not only employs the tactic of open warfare against us (1 Peter 5:8), but also uses the device of camouflage (2 Cor. 11:14). He disguises himself to deceive men about themselves, about the purpose of life, about eternity.

It is in this way that we are tempted still—more by the wiles of Satan than by his open assaults; more by the deceitfulness of sin than by its declared war. And it is little matter for wonder that those who succeed at Jericho and Ai fall into the nets woven and laid down by the wiles of Gibeon (F. B. Meyer, *Joshua: And the Land of Promise*, Revell, pp. 103-104).

The second and primary reason for Israel's failure is that the nation's leaders did not seek direction from God. "The Israelites were guilty of excessive credulity and culpable negligence, in not asking by the high priest's Urim and Thummim the mind of God, before entering into the alliance" (Jamieson, Fausset, & Brown, *A Commentary on the Old and New Testaments*, II, p. 25).

Did Joshua and his men think the evidence to be so beyond question that they needed no advice from Jehovah? Did they consider the matter too routine or unimportant to bother God about? Whatever the cause, it was a mistake to trust their own judgment and make their own plans. It still is.

Before entering into any alliance—taking a partner in life, going into business with another, yielding assent to any proposition which involves confederation with others —be sure to ask counsel at the mouth of the Lord. He will assuredly answer by an irresistible impulse—by the voice of a friend; by a circumstance strange and unexpected;

by a passage of Scripture. He will choose His own messenger; but He will send a message (Meyer, *Joshua,* p. 108).

2. Discovery of the ruse (vv. 16-17). Within a few days, Israel learned that they had been taken in. The Gibeonites lived in Canaan proper, about 20 miles from Gilgal, and not in some far country. An exploratory force confirmed the fraud by discovering the nearby location of Gibeon and its three dependent cities.

"A lying tongue is only for a moment" (Prov. 12:19b). Sooner or later trickery and deceit are exposed and truth will out. Almost daily our newspapers confirm the fact that it is impossible for a person to cover up an evil scheme indefinitely. In the long run, it will be exposed.

A preacher once announced to his congregation that he would speak the next Sunday on lying. He requested the audience to read Mark 17 in preparation. The following week he asked how many had read the chapter suggested. About 20 people held up their hands. The preacher thundered, "You're the very ones I want to address—there isn't any Mark 17!"

3. Decision of the leaders (vv. 18-27). When they discovered they had been duped, the Israelites wanted to disregard the covenant and destroy the Gibeonites; but Joshua and his staff declared that the deception did not nullify the treaty. The agreement was sacred because it had been ratified in the name of the Lord God of Israel. To break it would bring down the wrath of God on Israel. Such a judgment from God came to pass during David's reign because Saul disregarded this agreement (2 Sam. 21:1-6).

Joshua and the princes were men of integrity who stood by their word. Though humiliated by what had transpired, they did not want to bring disgrace upon God and His people by breaking a sacred treaty. It has been said that Joshua and his generals were more careful about their testimony than some Christians are today.

Yet, though Israel would not go back on the pledge, the deceivers had to be punished. Joshua therefore addressed the Gibeonites, rebuking them for their dishonesty, and declaring that they were cursed to perpetual slavery. This slavery would take the form of being woodcutters and water-bearers for the Israelites. And to keep the Gibeonites' idolatry from defiling the religion of Israel, their work would be carried out in the tabernacle, a place where they would be exposed to the worship of the one true God.

Thus the very thing the Gibeonites hoped to retain, they lost. They desperately wanted to remain free men; in the end they became slaves. As some one has said, "Joshua tore the disguises from the backs of these emissaries and put chains on their hands."

But the curse became a blessing. It was on behalf of the Gibeonites that God worked a great miracle (Josh. 10:10-14). Later the tabernacle was pitched at Gibeon (2 Chron. 1:3); still later the Gibeonites (then called Nethinims) replaced the Levites in temple service (Ezra 2:43; 8:20).

Such is the grace of God. And He is still able to turn a curse into a blessing. While it is usually true that the natural consequences of our sin will have to run their course, God in grace not only forgives but also overrules our mistakes and brings blessing out of our sins.

Have you hastily entered into an alliance with a modern-day Gibeonite, only to discover later the gravity of your error? Then seek God's forgiveness and God's grace which can bring triumph out of tragedy and joy out of sorrow.

Defense of the Gibeonites (10:1-43)

1. The cause of the conflict (vv. 1-5). In Jerusalem, five miles south of Gibeon, near panic had seized Adoni-zedek the king, and for good reason. The treacherous surrender of the Gibeonite cities completed an arc beginning at Gilgal and extending through Jericho and Ai to a point just a few miles northwest of Jerusalem. The handwriting was on the wall—Jerusalem's security was being severely threatened. If the advances of Israel's armies continued without challenge, Jerusalem would soon be surrounded and captured.

The king of Jerusalem sent an urgent message therefore to four other kings of southern Canaan stressing the fact that Gibeon had made peace with Israel. This was a traitorous and punishable act, which could pave the way for other cities to surrender in like manner. It was a signal for the kings to take immediate action against Gibeon.

There was a quick response and little time elapsed before the united force of a southern confederacy was laying siege to Gibeon.

2. The course of the conflict (vv. 6-15). Faced with certain slaughter, the Gibeonites sent a runner to Gilgal with an insistent appeal: "Come up to us quickly and save us and help us, for all the kings of the Amorites that live in the hill country have assembled against us."

Why should Joshua respond to this cry for help from the very people who had deceived him? Why not just sit back and let the Canaanites fight among themselves? The Israelites could then be rid of evidence of an embarrassing failure.

That this was not an option for Joshua is made clear by his immediate reaction. The reason for Joshua's response lay in the area of military strategy. Up to this time Israel's army attacked one fortified city at a time, at best a long and drawn out offensive procedure for conquering the entire land of Canaan. But now Joshua sensed he had the strategic break he needed. The combined Amorite armies of southern Canaan were camped in an open field outside Gibeon. An Israelite victory would break the enemy forces of the entire region.

Gathering his forces, Joshua and his men marched the 25 miles from Gilgal to Gibeon under cover of darkness. It was a tiresome journey with an ascent of 4,000 feet, up steep and difficult terrain. There was no opportunity to rest. The army was fatigued and faced a powerful foe. If God did not intervene, all would be lost.

Animated by God's promise of victory, Joshua led a surprise attack on the Amorite armies of the south, possibly while it was still dark. Panic seized the enemy and after a short stand in which many were killed, they broke and fled in wild confusion toward the west. Their escape route led through a narrow pass and down the Valley of Aijalon, with the Israelites in hot pursuit. This great highroad which led down from the central hill country has frequently been the scene of rout, as for example in A.D. 66 when the Roman general Cestius Gallus fled down this descent from the Jews.

The Amorites however did not escape. Using the forces of nature to fight for Israel, the Lord caused large hailstones to fall on the enemy with such deadly precision that more were killed in this way than by the sword.

This entire passage provides a striking illustration of the interplay between the human and divine factors in achieving victory. The narrative alternates between Joshua and Jehovah, and the parts each played in the conflict. The people were expected to fight, but God gave the victory. Certainly there are occasions when we can do nothing but wait for God to act; but usually we are to do our part with dependence on God to do His.

The Lord doesn't usually work a miracle for a lazy student at examination time, or for a slovenly housekeeper when unexpected visitors knock on the door of a disordered house, nor for a careless bookkeeper when the auditors arrive. God is always sufficient, and miracles will come when weakness needs them, but God will not usually do for us what we can and ought to do for ourselves (*Bible Knowledge,* Scripture Press, March 1972, p. 74).

As the day of the Battle of Beth-horon wore on, Joshua knew that the pursuit of the enemy would be long and arduous. At the most the military leader had 12 hours of daylight ahead of him, and he clearly needed much more if he was to realize the fulfillment of God's promise and see the total annihilation of his foes. Joshua therefore brought a most unusual request to the Lord: "O Sun, stand still at Gibeon, and O Moon in the Valley of Aijalon."

It was noon and the hot sun was directly overhead when Joshua uttered this prayer. The moon was on the horizon to the west. And the petition was quickly answered by the Lord: "So the sun stood still, and the moon stopped, until the nation avenged themselves of their enemies."

The record of this miracle has been considered a striking incident of Scripture and science being at variance. As we know, the sun does not move around the earth causing day and night. Rather the light and darkness come because the earth rotates on its axis in relation to the sun. In addressing the sun rather than the earth, Joshua was simply using the language of observation; he was speaking from the perspective and appearance of things on earth. And men still do the same thing, even in the scientific community. Scientists record the hours of sunrise and sunset, yet no one accuses them of scientific error.

Joshua's long day, however, must be explained. What actually did happen on that strange day? The answers are numerous. In fact, a research paper written by a seminary student discussed 12 explanations and stated these were only representative samples.

The explanation that does the most justice to the text is that in answer to Joshua's prayer, God caused the rotation of the earth to slow down so that it made one full rotation in 48 hours rather than in 24.

There would have been cataclysmic effects if the earth had stood still—everything loose would have been thrown into space, and monstrous tidal waves would have pounded the planet. Evidence that the earth's rotation simply slowed down is found in the closing words of verse 13. "And so the sun stopped in the middle of the sky, and did not hasten to go down for about a whole day." The sun was thus abnormally slow in setting; that is, its progression from noon to dusk was markedly lethargic.

On May 7, 1973 *The Dallas Morning News* reported: "A

giant storm on the sun last year probably slowed down the spinning of the earth for one rather long day." According to two scientists, this happened on August 4, 1972. Concluded the article: "The length of day on any planet is governed by the time it takes to complete one full rotation. The faster it rotates, the shorter the day. So the earth must have slowed down fractionally."

In Joshua's time just such a thing happened, extending that remarkable day by another 24 hours, giving Joshua and his soldiers sufficient time to complete their victorious battle.

An important fact that should not be overlooked is that the sun and moon were principal deities among the Canaanites. It may have seemed to the Canaanites that their gods were compelled to obey when the leader of the Israelites prayed.

The secret of Israel's triumph over the coalition of Canaanites is found in the words, "the Lord fought for Israel" (v. 14b). In answer to prayer, Israel experienced the dramatic intervention of God, and victory was assured.

While Joshua's prolonged day was a miraculous event not to be repeated, God still hearkens to the voice of man. He still responds to the cry of need and intervenes on behalf of His children.

Just before V-E Day of World War II, a soldier named Joel wrote his mother in New Jersey about the miraculous deliverance of his platoon.

Our outfit has been taken off the army's secret list so now you will hear a little of our activities. We are a part of the Third Army under General Patton. My platoon has been working mostly in observation posts and also a few patrols.

One of my best buddies, Tom, with his whole platoon was pinned down by German mortar and artillery fire. They were given the order to move, but couldn't because the Germans had full view of them from a hill and were zeroing their fire in on them perfectly.

Tom is the most conscientious Christian boy I have

ever met in the service. He knew something had to be done to save the 50 men. He crawled from his foxhole and looked things over. Seeing how things were, he lay down behind a tree and earnestly prayed God to help them out of this situation.

This is true, Mother. . . . After he prayed, a fog or mist rolled down between the two hills and the whole platoon got out of their foxholes and escaped. They reorganized in a little town behind the lines where there was a church building. They all went in and knelt down to pray and thank the Lord. Then they asked the kid to take the service.

That is true, Ma, and it just shows how much prayer can mean—if that wasn't an answer to prayer, I don't know what is. You can bet that Tom is respected by his buddies. ("The Miracle of the Fog," Good News Publisher).

3. The culmination of the conflict (vv. 16-43). Taking every advantage of the extended day, Joshua continued in hot pursuit of the enemy. The five strong kings and their armies had left their fortified cities to fight Israel in the open, and now Joshua was determined to prevent their return behind those walls. When word came that the kings had hidden in a cave, Joshua did not stop to deal with them but vigorously pursued the Amorite soldiers, killing all who did not escape to fortified cities. Then returning to the guarded cave, he brought out the captured kings. Following an Eastern custom often pictured on Egyptian and Assyrian monuments, Joshua instructed his field commanders to put their feet on the kings' necks. This was a symbol of the complete subjugation of the defeated enemy and a token of the future victories in Canaan. "For thus the Lord will do to all your enemies with whom you fight." After the kings were killed, their bodies were exposed by hanging until sundown, when they were thrown into the cave which was then blocked by great stones. Thus we have another memorial of Israel's victorious march through Canaan.

Early in his Christian experience, the believer recognizes that he too faces not a single foe but a coalition of the world, the flesh, and the devil. Without the help of God, victory is impossible.

A notorious drunkard was converted during the Welsh revival, and became a sober and respectable man. But the taverner was disturbed over losing such a good customer. One day as the Christian walked by, the proprietor called out, "What's gone wrong, Charlie? Why do you keep going past instead of coming in?"

Charlie stopped for a moment, and then with a glance heavenward, he replied, "Sir, it is not just that *I* keep going past; *we* go past!" And that's the secret of victory—the Lord is present and fights for us. "If God is for us, who is against us?" (Rom. 8:31)

The defeat of the five kings and their armies sealed the doom of southern Canaan. In a series of lightninglike raids, Joshua attacked the key military centers to destroy any further military capability. First, Joshua took Makkedah, Libnah, Lachish, and Eglon. These cities, ranging roughly from north to south, guarded the approaches to the southern highlands. Later, both Sennacherib and Nebuchadnezzar would follow the same strategy in their attacks on Judah.

Joshua next drove into the heart of the southern region and defeated its two chief walled cities, Hebron and Debir.

But Jerusalem, one of the five confederates, was bypassed. The troops may have been too weary to undertake this difficult task as they returned to camp at Gilgal. At any rate this pagan island in the land would be troublesome to the tribes of Judah and Benjamin until it was conquered by David (2 Sam. 5:7).

After a geographic summary of the extent of Israel's campaign in the south, the writer of the Book of Joshua concluded with a statement that gave credibility to the impressive sweep of victories recorded in this chapter: "And Joshua captured all these kings and their lands at one time, because the Lord the God of Israel, fought for Israel" (v. 42).

With such confidence Joshua and his tired armies returned to Gilgal to make preparations for the completion of their task.

When Mark Twain was traveling in Europe with his young daughter, he was feted in several cities by royalty and famed people in the arts and sciences. Toward the end of their journeys, his daughter said to him, "Papa, you know everybody but God, don't you?"

Joshua was a man who knew God above all else. The results are impressively recorded here. As Daniel later wrote, "The people who know their God will display strength and take action" (Dan. 11:32b).

For Joshua, for Daniel, and for you, knowing God and trusting Him implicitly is the key to victory.

8
Vanquishing
Enemies

Joshua 11-12

Near the end of his illustrious career, Sir Winston Churchill was invited back to his preparatory school to address the young men. Before Sir Winston arrived, the headmaster said to the students, "In a few days the prime minister will be here. Since he is one of the greatest orators of all time, I would challenge you to listen very carefully and take extensive notes on what this great man will say."

The day arrived. After an effusive introduction, Mr. Churchill stepped to the podium and delivered his address. He said, "Young gentlemen, never give up. Never give up. Never, never, never, never!" Then he sat down, for that was the sum total of his address. But who in that audience would ever forget Churchill's words?

Joshua was a man who exemplified that kind of spirit. With relentless perseverance, he pursued the goal of vanquishing the Canaanites and possessing the land of promise. After the exhausting military campaign in the south, he did not enjoy any prolonged period of recuperation before facing an even greater challenge, a massive coalition of forces in the north. But he was equal to the task.

Israel's leader was both a military genius and a spiritual

giant. Regarding his military capabilities Professor Kaufmann has noted:

> The conduct of the wars bespeaks a commander's personality. Joshua does not fight a single defensive war. All his wars are offensive. He does not dig in in fortified positions: in all his encounters he employs field warfare. When he learns that an attack is impending, he anticipates it by an attack of his own. He exploits the factor of surprise. In a night march he climbs to the position of the kings besieging Gibeon and falls upon them suddenly (10:9). He also falls suddenly upon the kings in their gathering at the waters of Merom (11:6). The flight of his own army before Ai is immediately exploited by him for a tactical purpose: he stages a decoy-rout. He makes consummate use of the topographical factor [at Ai]. . . . The rout of the Canaanites in the battle for Gibeon is exploited by Joshua with consummate skill. From his provisional camp near Makkedah (10:21), he sends units to harry the retreating enemy. He does not let his troops rest: the Canaanites must be prevented from reaching their cities. . . . Here too, then, we see the true touch of a great commander (*The Biblical Account of the Conquest of Palestine*, Magnus Press, Hebrew University, pp. 96-97).

Spiritually, Joshua served as an example to the people: he stood by the promise the spies made to Rahab; he kept faith with the deceptive Gibeonites; he could have used his position for personal gain but he did not.

With such a leader at the helm of affairs in Israel, the conquest entered its final phase. Total victory was assured.

The Victory in the North (11:1-15)

The alarm of the northern Canaanite kings was aroused by Joshua's crushing victories in the south. Jabin, king of Hazor, organized a last desperate attempt to stop the conquest of the land by the armies of Israel. No doubt his attempt would have had a better chance of success if he had joined the coalition of Adoni-zedek, marching in force from the north to merge with the southern armies to crush Israel at Gibeon. But God restrained Jabin from that move and now he reacted to the crisis with dispatch and near panic.

1. The confederation (vv. 1-5). Messengers fanned out rapidly in all directions, north, south, east, and west, with an urgent call to arms. It may have been quite similar to the summons Saul issued later to Israel to follow him to Jabesh-gilead. Saul killed a yoke of oxen and sent pieces of the animals by couriers who cried, "Whoever does not come out after Saul and after Samuel, so shall it be done to his oxen" (1 Sam. 11:7).

Although there was no love lost between these kings of the north, the threat of annihilation forced them into an alliance. They joined forces a few miles northwest of the Sea of Galilee in a plain near the waters of Merom.

The combined army was impressive. Not only did it include soldiers in number "as the sand that is on the seashore," but in addition boasted of horses and chariots in great numbers. Josephus, the Jewish historian who lived in the first century A.D., speculated that this northern confederacy included 300,000 infantry soldiers, 10,000 cavalry troops, and 20,000 chariots.

The odds against the Israelites seemed overwhelming. How could Joshua hope to win this battle?

2. The conflict (vv. 6-15). The vast host of Canaanites were pitched at the waters of Merom. It was probably their plan, after organizing their detachments and adopting a strategy to sweep down the Jordan Valley and attack Joshua at Gilgal. But Joshua did not wait for the battle to come to him; he was in fact already marching toward Merom, a five-day trek from home base. And as he marched he had a lot of time to think about the immense array awaiting him. No doubt he trembled at the prospect of the battle that loomed before him.

Then God spoke. The promise He gave to Joshua was unmistakably clear: "Do not be afraid because of them, for tomorrow at this time I will deliver all of them slain before Israel." As with God's promises to us, this one was clear, definite, concrete. It was just what Joshua needed and Israel's leader took the promise at face value, believing that God would give them a victory over their formidable foe.

The battle took place in two phases. The very next day Joshua surprised the enemy, attacking them at the waters of Merom and chasing them westward to the coast (to Sidon and Misrephoth-maim), and eastward to the valley of Mizpeh. Following God's directions to the letter, Joshua killed all of the enemy, burned the chariots, and lamed the horses.

But why did God command such drastic actions as burning the chariots and hamstringing the horses? Because the Canaanites used horses in their pagan worship. Also there was danger that Israel might trust in these new weapons of war rather than in the Lord. The psalmist declared, "Some boast in chariots, and some in horses; but we will boast in the name of the Lord, our God" (Ps. 20:7).

Perhaps the horses and chariots might have been to Israel what nuclear power is to our own nation. Can superior nuclear weaponry be an absolute guarantee of security? Do we really live by what we declare on our coinage, "IN GOD WE TRUST"? Or must we also add, "Provided we are ahead in the arms race"? Where do we really place our trust?

In the second phase of the conflict in northern Canaan, Joshua returned after routing the enemy army, and captured all the cities of the defeated kings. Hazor, however, was singled out for special treatment, probably because it was by far the largest city of ancient Palestine, 14 times larger than Megiddo, and 25 times larger than Jericho. Occupying a position of immense strategic importance, Hazor dominated several branches of an ancient highway which led from Egypt to Syria and on to Assyria and Babylon. Hazor alone among the northern cities was both seized and burned. While Joshua may have decided to save the other captured cities for later Israelite use, he determined to make an example of Hazor, capital of all these city-states and the convener of their armies. If great Hazor could not escape, the Canaanites would be forced to acknowledge that any city could be burned if Joshua so decreed.

Thus a decisive victory was won in the north. And the key was obedience to God. "Just as the Lord had commanded Moses His servant, so Moses commanded Joshua, and so Joshua did; he left nothing undone of all that the Lord had commanded Moses."

Marshall Foch, in the second battle of the Marne during World War I, was asked about his situation. He sent back this dispatch: "My left falters. My center is weak. My right crumbles. I am attacking."

Joshua too was always attacking—because those were his orders. But those orders included the total extermination of the Canaanite people of the land, an extreme measure which has caused some to reject this so-called "notorious Book of Joshua" and to characterize the God who ordered such barbaric acts as "a Holy Terror."

In response to such reactions it needs to be reaffirmed that responsibility for the destruction of the Canaanites does rest squarely with God and not with the Israelites, who simply carried out His orders. (See Deut. 20:16-17.)

Let sinful people and nations take note that God does not countenance sin indefinitely. History clearly demonstrates this.

The Canaanites were not the last people to taste God's wrath. Bloody Assyria, sensual Babylon, vice-ridden Greece, degenerate Rome have each been consumed by the results of their own lust. Later ages saw the decline of Spain with its Inquisition and more recently the collapse of the sadistic Third Reich. The greatest nations in the world today are by no means immune from God's punishing hand—and neither is any individual who dares to sin deliberately against the will and purpose of the sovereign Lord of the earth" (*Bible Knowledge*, Scripture Press, March 1972, p. 83).

In 1863, Abraham Lincoln issued the following proclamation: We have been the recipients of the choicest bounties of heaven. We have been preserved, these many years in peace and prosperity. We have grown in numbers, wealth, and power as no other nation has ever grown, but we have forgotten God. We have forgotten the gracious hand which preserved us in peace, and multiplied and enriched and strengthened us; and we have vainly imagined, in the deceitfulness of our hearts, that all these blessings were produced by some superior wisdom and virtue of our own. Intoxicated with unbroken success, we have become too self-sufficient to feel the necessity of redeeming and preserving grace, too proud to pray to the God that made us: It behooves us, then, to humble ourselves before the offended Power, to confess our national sins, and to pray for clemency and forgiveness.

These are warnings which apply to America in the 1980s, and words we would do well to heed.

The Conquest Summarized (11:16—12:24)

Victory in the north brought about the formal end of the conquest. Before recording how the land was apportioned among the tribes, the author paused to review and summarize the scope of the triumph by Israel in Canaan. Included is a description of the conquered geographic areas (11:16-23) and a list of the defeated kings (12:1-24).

1. The conquered areas (11:16-23). The battles fought by Joshua and his troops ranged over lands that stretched from border to border, from south to north and from east to west. The period of conquest lasted a long time, and victory did not come easily or quickly—it rarely does. Yet in all of the military confrontations, only Gibeon sought peace. The other cities were taken in battle, God having hardened their hearts to fight Israel so that they might be destroyed. The Canaanites' day of grace was gone. They had sinned against the light of the revelation of God in nature, in conscience, and in His recent miraculous works at the Red Sea, the Jordan River, and Jericho. Now the sovereign God confirmed the hearts of these unrepentant men in their stubborn unbelief before judging them.

Special mention is made of the Anakim, the giants who had terrified the spies 40 years before, of whom it had been said, "Who can stand before the sons of Anak?" (Deut. 9:2) These supposedly invincible foes were utterly destroyed. None remained except some in the remote cities of Gaza, Gath, and Ashdod. That proved to be an unfortunate omission on Joshua's part—in David's time Goliath came from Gath to defy Israel and her God.

The section concludes with a declaration that summarizes the Book of Joshua as a whole. "So Joshua took the whole land, according to all that the Lord had spoken to Moses, and Joshua gave it for an inheritance to Israel according to their division by their tribes. Thus the land had rest from war." This verse looks back to the conquest, in chapters 1—11 and forward to the distribution of the land, in chapters 13—22.

But how are we to understand the statement that "Joshua took the whole land," when we are soon to read that "very much of the land remains to be possessed" (13:1)? To the Hebrew mind the part stands for the whole. It thus only needs to be demonstrated that Joshua took key centers in all parts of the land to validate the statement that he had conquered the whole land. In an article appearing in the *Concordia Theological Monthly* ("Universalism and the Conquest of Canaan," 35:1, pp. 8-17, January 1964), A. J. Mattill, Jr. meticulously analyzed the conquest of Canaan by surveying the geographical divisions of the land and the representative parts of it subdued by Joshua. Included were conquered sites on the coastal plain, the shephelah (foothills), the central plateau, the Jordan Valley, and the Transjordan plateau. No area was totally bypassed. Joshua did indeed take the whole land, or the land as a whole, just as God promised he would if he followed the divine Word rather than human wisdom (Josh. 1:8).

Joshua's accomplishments were notable, even against tremendous odds, because he trusted in God, Richard Halverson challenges us to a similar exercise of faith:

When the situation is hopeless . . . That's *the time for faith!* Actually there is *no such thing as a hopeless situation* for one who trusts in God . . . But the fact is that most of us turn to God *only when we think the situation's hopeless.* As long as we can find something in our circumstances on which to pin our hope *we trust that possibility* rather than God. Until we *have used up all our options*—see no shred of hope in our circumstances . . . Then—*as a last resort*—we may turn to God. Someone put it this way: "As long as we have reason for hope, we hope in the reason." As long as we can think up possible answers—*we depend upon human ingenuity*—or luck—or coincidence—etc. Then, when *alternatives are exhausted* and there is nowhere else to turn . . . We *give God His chance.* How much better to *trust God no matter what! (Perspective,* Sept. 28, 1977).

Joshua trusted God "no matter what!"

2. The conquered kings (12:1-24). Concluding the story begun in Joshua 1 is a detailed catalog of the kings defeated by Israel. The preceding chapters list the major battles. Only in Joshua 12 is a complete list of conquered kings. Israel did not occupy all of these cities, for Joshua did not have sufficient manpower to leave a controlling garrison in each place. But the defensive strength of each city was broken. Joshua no doubt reasoned that the actual occupation by the respective tribes should not be too difficult to carry out.

Joshua 12:1-6 records the victories under Moses on the east side of Jordan (Num. 21; Deut. 2:24—3:17). The defeated cities on the west side of the river are listed in 12:7-24. In this section the kings of southern Canaan are first enumerated (vv. 9-16) and then the kings of northern Canaan (vv. 17-24).

It is surprising to find 31 kings in a land 150 miles from north to south, and 50 miles from east to west. But it must be remembered that these kings reigned over city-states and only had a local authority. Apart from the confederations that were formed by the kings of Jerusalem and Hazor, the lack of a central government in Canaan made the task of the Israelites somewhat easier than it might have been otherwise.

Reflecting on the significance of Joshua's victories one writer has stated, "There has never been a greater war for a greater cause. The battle of Waterloo decided the fate of Europe, but this series of contests in far-off Canaan decided the fate of the world" (Henry T. Sell, *Bible Study by Periods:* Revell, p. 83).

The ancient conflict in Canaan is significant also because it symbolizes the spiritual warfare of the Christian, a warfare that is constant and intense.

John Bunyan in *Pilgrim's Progress* describes how the Interpreter conducted Christian to where he beheld a stately palace on the top of which were walking certain persons clothed all in gold. Around the door stood a great company of men desirous to go in, but who dared not. A little distance from the door, at a table, sat a man with a book and an inkhorn to take the name of him that would enter into the palace. In the doorway stood many men in armor to keep it, being resolved to do what hurt and mischief they could do to anyone who tried to enter. All were standing back in fear, and Christian himself was in a maze, when he saw a man of stout countenance go up to him with the inkhorn and say, " 'Set down my name, sir'; the which when he had done, he saw the man draw his sword, and put a helmet on his head, and rush toward the door upon the armed men." After receiving and giving many wounds, he cut his way into the palace; and voices were heard of those who walked in gold raiment on top of the palace, saying, "Come in, come in, Eternal glory thou shalt win."

For the Christian it is indeed "drawn swords to the very

gates of heaven." But victory is possible along the way. We need only follow the example of Israel's leader, Joshua, who believed in God—

    taking Him at His Word,
    trusting His promises,
    relying on His presence.

As a result, he vanquished his enemies.

"This is the victory that has overcome the world, our faith" (1 John 5:4b).

9
The Divine
Realtor at Work

Joshua 13-17

"You are old and advanced in years." That was God's announcement to Joshua. Does anyone like to be reminded that old age has come? Yet however much we want to retain the feeling of youth, our time will come. "You are old"—What solemn words to hear. Life has flown by so rapidly and now is almost past.

In his will, John Bacon, an 18th-century English sculptor, ordered a marker for his grave with the following inscription: "What I was as an artist seemed to me of some importance while I lived; what I really was as a believer in Christ Jesus is the only thing of importance to me now."

Sensing death was near, a faithful pastor said to his family from his sickbed,

I am ready to go. I have had a good life. The Lord has been so good. I'm thankful for a wonderful wife. I'm thankful for my family. I am thankful for over 40 years of ministry. I did not do a lot of great things in life, but I was able to touch a life here, and touch a life there for God, and that's what it's all about. I have done the will of God. That's what really counts.

Joshua too had been a good and faithful servant, and it

does not seem that he reacted with chagrin or pain to the announcement that he would not complete the work to which he had given so much.

It was not that Joshua would now drop into oblivion, having successfully removed the major military threats to Israel's survival in Canaan. Rather, Joshua the soldier would now give way to Joshua the administrator. The land conquered by bloody warfare must be assigned to the various tribes, and Joshua would oversee this important transaction. It would be a less exhausting service, and one more suited to his advancing years.

This section of the Book of Joshua seems tedious, with its detailed lists of boundaries and cities. Someone suggested that most of this long section reads like a real estate deed. And that is precisely what we have in these lengthy narrations, legal descriptions of the areas allocated to the 12 tribes. Title deeds are important documents and should not be regarded as insignificant or superfluous.

Also, we need to remember that this was a climactic moment in the life of the young nation. After centuries in Egyptian bondage, decades in the barren wilderness, years of hard fighting in Canaan, the hour had arrived when the Israelites could at last settle down to build homes, cultivate the soil, raise families, and live in peace in their own land. The day of land allotment must have been a happy day indeed!

The Divine Command to Divide the Land (13:1-7)

"Now therefore apportion this land for an inheritance to the nine tribes, and the half-tribe of Manasseh" God thus directed Joshua to divide the land west of the Jordan.

Since Joshua died at the age of 110, (24:29), he was probably at least 100 by this time. And the commission of Joshua had included not only the conquest of the land but also its distribution to the tribes. He therefore needed to move on quickly to this new assignment.

The task of allocation would take place at once, even

though there remained much land to possess. The unconquered lands are listed from south to north and include what we know as Philistia, Phoenicia, and Lebanon. God promised to drive out the inhabitants of these areas, and Joshua was to allot them now, even though they were still occupied.

The work of conquest that Joshua had begun would therefore be finished by someone else. Perhaps he needed to be reminded that this grand operation was not his, but God's.

William Blaikie observed,

God is not limited to one instrument, or to one age, or to one plan. Never does Providence appear to us so strange, as when a noble worker is cut down in the very midst of his work. A young missionary has just shown his splendid capacity for service, when fever strikes him low, and in a few days all that remains of him is rotting in the ground. "What can God mean?" we sometimes ask impatiently. "Does He not know the rare value and the extreme scarcity of such men, that He sets them up apparently just to throw them down?" . . . But He is not limited to single agents. When Stephen died, He raised up Saul. For Wycliffe He gave Luther. When George Wishart was burnt He raised up John Knox. . . . So Joshua must be content to have done his part, and done it well, although he did not conquer all the land, and there yet remained much to be possessed" (*The Book of Joshua*, Hodder & Stoughton, pp. 253-54).

The Special Grant to the Eastern Tribes 13:8-33)

Joshua was next called on to recognize and confirm what had already been done by Moses on the east side of the Jordan. The tribes of Reuben, Gad, and the half-tribe of Manasseh possessed large herds of cattle, and were anxious to settle in the rich grazing lands of Transjordan. Only when the men accepted the challenge to fight alongside their brothers to win Canaan proper did Moses agree to the assignment.

Reuben received the territory previously occupied by

Moab, east of the Dead Sea. Gad's inheritance, in the center of the region, was in the original land of Gilead. The allotment to the half-tribe of Manasseh was the rich tableland of Bashan east of the Sea of Galilee.

With regard to Reuben's portion, it should be noted that centuries before the land was divided, the dying Jacob had uttered prophecies regarding his sons. Concerning his firstborn Reuben he said, "Reuben, you are my firstborn; my might, and the beginning of my strength, preeminent in dignity, and preeminent in power. Uncontrolled as water, you shall not have preeminence, because you went up to your father's bed; then you defiled it—he went up to my couch" (Gen. 49:3-4; see Gen. 35:22). Though he was the firstborn and entitled to a double portion (Deut. 21:17), neither he or his tribe received it. Now after more than three centuries, the punishment for Reuben's sinful deed was passed on to his descendants; the right of the firstborn passed over to his brother Joseph who received two portions, one for Ephraim and the other for Manasseh.

But was the request of the two and one-half tribes to settle in Transjordan a wise one? History would seem to answer No. Their territories had no natural boundaries to the east and were therefore constantly exposed to invasion by the Moabites, Canaanites, Syrians, Midianites, Amalekites, and others. And when the king of Assyria looked covetously toward Canaan, the two and one-half tribes were the first to be carried into captivity by the Assyrian armies. (See 1 Chron. 5:26.)

By contrast with the rich though dangerous inheritance of these tribes, the tribe of Levi received no inheritance from Moses. At first this might seem puzzling, but closer examination reveals that in lieu of territorial possessions, the tribe of Levi was allotted the sacrifices or offerings (Josh. 13:14), the priesthood (18:7), and the Lord Himself (13:33). Who could dream of a greater inheritance?

The two and one-half tribes chose, as Lot did, on the basis

of appearance, and their inheritance was ultimately lost to them. On the other hand the Levites, requesting no portion, were given an inheritance of abiding spiritual significance.

This reminds us of the words of Jesus, "Do not lay up for yourselves treasures upon earth, where moth and rust destroy, and where thieves break in and steal. But lay up for yourselves treasures in heaven, where neither moth nor rust destroys, and where thieves do not break in or steal; for where your treasure is, there will your heart be also" (Matt. 6:19-21).

In the south of France, near the Mediterranean coast, one may see an old tombstone inscribed with these cryptic words: "HERE LIES THE SOUL OF COUNT LOUIS ESTER-FIELD." Year after year travelers passed the spot, paying little notice. One day a man stopped in front of the tombstone and began digging. At last he came upon a metal box and opening it found it was full of jewels and gold coins. And with them was this legal note: "You are my heir. To you I bequeath this wealth, to you who have understood. In this box is my soul—the money without which a man is but a machine and his life but a long procession of weary, empty years."

What folly! It is not money or the lack of it that makes the difference. Only a relationship with God and a priority on spiritual realities make life worth living.

The Special Gift to Caleb (14:1-15)
The account now turns to the distribution of the land in Canaan proper, to the remaining nine and one-half tribes. The land was to be divided by lot. The Lord had instructed Moses that each tribe was to receive territory proportionate to its population, with the casting of lots to determine the location (Num. 26:54-56). According to Jewish tradition, the name of a tribe and the boundary lines of a territory were simultaneously drawn from two urns. This method designated each tribal inheritance. But it was not a matter of blind chance that decided the tribal location, for God was superintending

the whole procedure. The inequities of assignments that existed, and caused some tensions and jealousies among the tribes, should have been accepted as a part of God's purpose and not as something that was arbitrary and unfair.

And so we too must accept our lot in life. Of course, there are inequities—in intelligence, physical appearance, talents, personality, and material possessions. We cannot hope to understand in this life the seeming unfairness and inequalities that exist. As Christians we know that our lot is not a matter of good or bad luck, but is precisely God's choice for us. Furthermore, we know that in the life to come we will fully understand all of the assignments God has made.

The time for the casting of lots arrived and the tribe of Judah, receiving the first portion, assembled at Gilgal before Joshua. Before the lots were cast, Caleb, the grand old man of Israel, stepped forward to remind Joshua of a promise the Lord made to him 45 years earlier: "To him and to his sons I will give the land on which he has set his foot because he has followed the Lord fully" (Deut. 1:36).

William Hunt, the noted painter, addressed a stern remark to a pupil one afternoon when the class was painting a glowing sunset. Looking over the boy's shoulder, the artist noticed to his dismay that the student had ignored the sunset and was busy painting an old red barn with decaying shingles. "Son, son," he shouted. "It won't be light long! You haven't time for both shingles and sunsets. You must choose!"

Caleb was an old man. Life was ebbing away and he had to make a choice. What did he yet want most of all? In a remarkable address to Joshua, he reviewed the highlights of his life and made his request.

1. Kadesh-barnea (vv. 6-9). Caleb is introduced in this passage as "the son of Jephunneh the Kenizzite," and we are informed in Genesis 15:19 that the Kenizzites were a tribe of Canaan in Abraham's day. Caleb's family then was originally outside the covenant and commonwealth of Israel, as were Heber the Kenite, Ruth the Moabitess, Uriah the Hittite, and others. It is apparent that the Kenizzites, in part at least, joined the tribe of Judah before the Exodus. Their faith was not then merely hereditary but was the fruit of conviction. And Caleb displayed that faith throughout his long lifetime.

Standing before General Joshua, his old friend and fellow spy, Caleb loquaciously told the story of that never-to-be forgotten day, 45 years earlier, when the two of them stood alone against the other 10 spies and the cowardly mob. Moses had sent 12 spies into Canaan, two of whom were Caleb and Joshua. When the spies returned, 10 of them praised the land itself, but fearfully concluded Israel could not conquer it. Caleb dared to disagree (Num. 13:30); and when the fears of the people threatened to bring national rebellion, Joshua joined his colleague in urging the people to trust God for victory (Num. 14:6-9). For his leadership against the unbelieving spies and people, God singled Caleb out for blessing and promised him a special reward (Num. 14:24; Deut. 1:36).

Caleb's testimony was simple. On that memorable day, he had spoken what was in his heart. It was not that he minimized the problems—the giants and the fortified cities—but that he magnified God. To him God was bigger than the biggest problem! *Caleb had faith in the power of God.*

Not so the other spies. They magnified the problems and in the process minimized God.

But Caleb would not follow the crowd. He did not once consider sacrificing his own convictions in order to make the majority report unanimous. Instead he followed the Lord God fully.

During World War II, German Pastor Martin Niemoller was imprisoned by the Nazis. Reflecting on his experience in those days he said,

First the Nazis came for the Communists, and I did not speak up, for I was not a Communist. Then the Nazis came for the Jews, and I did not speak up, for I was not a Jew. Then the Nazis came for the Trade Unionists and I did not speak up, for I was not a Trade Unionist. And then the Nazis came for the Catholics, and I did not speak up, for I was a Protestant. And then the Nazis came for me. By that time, there was no one left to speak up for anyone.

At Kadesh-barnea, Caleb spoke up for God. May we have courage to do the same even though we may be a part of a small minority.

2. *The wilderness and conquest (vv. 10-11).* Caleb reminisced about God's faithfulness to him over many years. First he affirmed that God had kept him alive the past 45 years as He promised. Actually Caleb was the recipient of two divine promises: one, that his life would be prolonged; and the other, that he would one day inherit the territory he had bravely explored near Hebron. Alexander Maclaren noted that "the daily fulfillment of the one fed the fire of his faith in the ultimate accomplishment of the other" (*Expositions of Holy Scripture*, Vol. 3, p. 162).

But 45 years is a long time to wait for the fulfillment of a pledge, a long time for faith to live on a promise. Yet wait he did, through the weary years of the wilderness wanderings and demanding years of the conquest.

Caleb had strong faith in the promises of God. They sustained him in difficult times. Such promises always will.

David Adeney testified, "I discovered the power of the Word of God in my own life during a time of depression when I was strongly tempted to give up. Almost in desperation, I turned to John's Gospel and read it all through at one sitting. God spoke to me through it and I realized again that faith comes through the hearing of the Word of Christ" (*His,* April 1980, p. 23).

Bible historians take note of Caleb's remarks in verse 10, since they enable us to determine the length of the conquest of Canaan by the Israelites. Caleb stated he was 40 years old when he went to spy out the land. The wilderness wanderings lasted 38 years, giving a total of 78. Caleb was now 85, which means the conquest lasted 7 years. This is confirmed by Caleb's reference in verse 10 to God's sustaining grace for 45 years since Kadesh-barnea—38 years of wandering plus 7 years of conquest.

There is deep tragedy here when we see that Israel could have possessed their homeland in about 8 years if they had responded in faith to Caleb and Joshua at Kadesh-barnea. Instead it took 45 years, for the unbelieving generation was sentenced to die in the wilderness. What price unbelief!

3. Hebron (vv. 12-15). Caleb concluded his speech to Joshua with an astounding request. At the age of 85, when he might have asked for a quiet place to spend his last days raising some vegetables or flowers, he requested instead the section that had struck fear into the hearts of the 10 spies. This was the inheritance he desired in fulfillment of God's earlier promise. And though old age is usually more anxious to talk about old conflicts than to take on new ones, Caleb was ready for one more good battle. He was eager to fight the Anakim at Hebron and take the city for his possession.

It has been said that you can always tell a man's size by the bigness or smallness of the thing he attacks. Caleb chose a large and foreboding task. Not that he was filled with pride in his own ability but rather that he believed God would be with him.

Caleb had faith in the presence of God. When he said, "Perhaps the Lord will be with me" he was expressing humility, not doubt. Then with flashing eyes and a strong voice he concluded, "I shall drive them out, as the Lord has spoken." And drive them out he did, as we read in Joshua 15:13-19.

Joshua's response to his old friend is captured in these imagined words:

Caleb, it's yours. You deserve it. I'm sorry I forgot! It is because of you that I mustered enough courage to stand against Israel's hostility and disobedience. It is because of you that I spoke out against their rebellion and unbelief. You helped me become the man that I am—a man that God could trust to lead Israel in place of Moses. I drew strength from you, Caleb. And you have been faithful to me. You never showed jealousy or resentment because you were not chosen to lead Israel—even though you were a stronger man than I, both physically and emotionally. I'm sorry I didn't remember God's promise myself. I'm glad you reminded me! It's yours! Take the mountain God promised you (Gene A. Getz, *Joshua,* Regal, p. 161).

When Caleb could have lived out the rest of his days in comfort and ease, he chose instead a hazardous but important mission. And in so doing he reminds us of many servants of Christ who have forsaken the comfortable life to go where God has directed. A notable example is William Borden whose life was capsulized by a Dallas Seminary student, as follows:

He couldn't have done anything else—or could he?

• While a student at Yale University, he was elected president of his Phi Beta Kappa chapter.

• At 20 he founded the effective Yale Hope Rescue Mission.

• Shortly after graduation from Princeton Seminary, he spoke to no fewer than 30 leading colleges and seminaries within a period of three months.

• He became a millionaire, as heir to the Borden dairy fortune.

So what did he decide to do with his life?

• He dedicated himself to reach the Moslems in an interior province of China. He went to Cairo to learn Arabic and to take studies in Islam in anticipation of this work. Within a few months he was dead from cerebral meningitis.

Why did he do this?

• He wrote: In every man's heart there is a throne and a cross. If Christ is on the throne, self is on the cross; and if self, even a little bit, is on the throne, Jesus is on the cross in that man's heart. . . . If Jesus is on the throne, you will go where He wants you to go.

• He prayed: Lord Jesus, I take hands off, as far as my life is concerned. I put Thee on the throne in my heart. Change, cleanse, use me as Thou shalt choose. I thank Thee.

Was it worth it?

• He did extensive tract distribution and personal work, and organized others to do the same.

• Through his death many dedicated themselves to carry the Gospel to those who had not heard it.

• His testimony has been greatly used among Moslems to show what Christian love led one man to do for them.

The Portion of the Tribe of Judah (15:1-63)

Caleb's request having been granted, the people returned to the business of dividing the land west of the Jordan among the nine and one-half tribes.

Judah was the first to receive an inheritance and as the largest tribe, their portion exceeded that of any of the others.

Jacob's prophecy regarding Judah and his seed was remarkably fulfilled in the land allotment after the conquest. (See Gen. 49:8-12.)

• Judah was surrounded by enemies. The Moabites were on the east, Edomites on the south, Amalekites to the southwest, and Philistines to the west. Thus hemmed in by fierce foes, Judah would need strong rulers, men like King David, to survive.

• The land allotted to Judah was ideally suited to the planting of vineyards. It was from a Judean valley that the spies cut down the gigantic cluster of grapes.

• Judah was the tribe from which Messiah would come. He would come as Shiloh, the Man of rest (Matt. 11:28), or the Peace-bringer (Isa. 9:6).

The borders of Judah are described in Joshua 15:1-12.

The southern boundary extended from the south end of the Dead Sea westward to the river of Egypt (Wadi el-Arish). The northern border extended from the north tip of the Dead Sea to the Mediterranean. These two bodies of water were the eastern and western limits. Composed mainly of the territory conquered by Joshua in his southern campaign (Josh. 10), the area included some fertile tracts, but large parts were mountainous and barren.

Included in Judah's portion was Hebron which had been granted to Caleb. The record now describes how that courageous warrior claimed and enlarged this inheritance, aided by a brave kinsman Othniel who became his son-in-law.

The cities of Judah are listed according to their location in the four main geographic regions of the tribe: the cities in the south or Negev (vv. 21-32); the cities in the western foothills or Shephelah (vv. 33-47); the cities in the central hill country (vv. 48-60); the cities in the sparsely populated wilderness of Judah which slopes down toward the Dead Sea (vv. 61-62).

Judah inherited well over 100 cities and seems to have occupied them with little or no difficulty, with the significant exception of Jerusalem. "As for the Jebusites, the inhabitants of Jerusalem, the sons of Judah could not drive them out" (v. 63).

Was it that the men of Judah *could not* because they *would not*? Was the failure due to a lack of strength or a lack of faith?

The account of Judah's inheritance ends on an ominous and foreboding note. Witherby concludes:

They could not drive them out! The note has been struck, its tone will increase in volume, it will repeat itself again and again, until the sound of victory be swallowed up in the cries of defeat and loss and in the wails of bondage and ruin (*The Book of Joshua,* H. Forbes Witherby, Loizeauz, p. 188).

The Portion of the Joseph Tribes (16:1—17:18)

The powerful house of Joseph, made up the tribes of Ephraim and Manasseh, inherited the rich territory of central Canaan. Because Joseph kept the family alive during the famine in Egypt, the patriarch Jacob ordained that the two sons of Joseph, Ephraim and Manasseh, should be made founders and heads of tribes with their uncles (Gen. 48:5). Their lot in Canaan was in many respects the most beautiful and fertile.

1. The tribe of Ephraim (16:4-10). Located immediately north of the territory to be assigned to Dan and Benjamin, Ephraim's allotment stretched from the Jordan to the Mediterranean. It included the sites of some of Joshua's battles, as well as Shiloh, where the tabernacle would remain for some 300 years. To encourage unity, some of Ephraim's cities were located in the territory of Manasseh.

But the men of Ephraim, like those of Judah, did not completely drive out the Canaanites from their region. Motivated by a materialistic attitude, they chose to put the Canaanites under tribute to gain additional wealth. And that proved to be a fatal mistake. For in later centuries, in the time of the Judges, the arrangement was reversed as the Canaanites rose up and enslaved the Israelites.

In addition to the historical lesson there is a spirtual principle here. It is all too easy to tolerate and excuse some pet sin in our lives, only to wake up someday to the grim realization that it has risen up to possess us and drive us to spiritual defeat. It pays to deal with sin decisively and harshly.

2. The tribe of Manasseh (17:1-13). The descendants of the firstborn of Manasseh settled in Transjordan. The remaining heirs settled in Canaan proper and were given the territory north of Ephraim extending also from the Jordan River to the Mediterranean Sea.

Special note was taken of the daughters of Zelophehad. Because the father died without sons, the Lord had declared that in this and other such cases the daughters could receive the inheritance (Num. 27:1-11). They now claimed and received their portion within the territory of Manasseh. The incident is not without significance, for it shows a concern for women, at a time when most societies regarded them as mere chattel.

Several cities located in the tribes of Issachar and Asher were given to Manasseh. These were the Canaanite fortresses of Bethshean, Ibleam, Dor, Endor, Taanach, and Megiddo. Apparently it was considered necessary for military purposes that these cities be held by a strong tribe. The decision however was in vain for the sons of Manasseh, like the Ephraimites, chose tribute over triumph.

3. The complaint of Ephraim and Manasseh, (vv. 14-18). The sons of Joseph registered a belligerent complaint with Joshua, claiming that their allotment was too small, in light of their large population. With tact and firmness, Joshua challenged them first to clear the trees and settle in the forested hill country. Then they should combine their energies to drive out the Canaanites.

But this is not what they wanted to hear. Francis Schaeffer comments:

> The people of God did not go on to do what God told them to do for two reasons. First, they wanted peace at any cost and in spite of God's commands; second, they wanted wealth. They were practical materialists. For sake of ease and money, they did not go forward and do what God told them to do. . . . We Christians stand in the same danger. It is all too easy to fail to possess the possessions God has promised because we either draw back out of fear of the troubles that being a Christian will bring us or we become caught up in the affluent society where people sail their little boats upon this plastic culture (*Joshua and the Flow of Biblical History,* InterVarsity Press, pp. 157-58, 162).

Better by far that we follow a Caleb, whose life commitment was to do the will of God, regardless of cost to peace

and possessions, to the very end. His vision and purpose seem
to be well enunciated in the poem of Amy Carmichael (*Amy
Carmichael of Dohnavur*, F. Houghton, p. 366).

> Make us Thy mountaineers;
> We would not linger on the lower slope,
> Fill us afresh with hope, O God of hope,
> That undefeated we may climb the hill
> As seeing Him who is invisible.
> Let us die climbing. When this little while
> Lies far behind us, and the last defile
> Is all alight, and in that light we see
> Our Leader and our Lord, what will it be?

10
God's Inheritance - No One Left out

Joshua 18-21

Quitting is easy. Anybody can say, "The hill is too high," or "It's too far away." Anybody can say, "I'm tired," or "I'm bored," or "I'm scared."

Whenever you begin a difficult task, don't stop in the middle. See the thing through!

Israel stopped in the middle. Although much of Canaan had been allocated, seven tribes were still without a home, and apparently were content to continue a nomadic and purposeless existence. Their listlessness provoked Joshua to prod them into action.

The Portions of the Remaining Tribes (18:1—19:48)

Before the final divisions of the land were made, the Israelites moved en masse from Gilgal to Shiloh, from the Jordan Valley to the hill country. Shiloh was located in the center of the land; and in this central and convenient location, the tabernacle was erected.

The dissatisfaction of the sons of Joseph with their allotment was an ominous foreshadowing of the future disintegration of the nation because of self-interest. To counteract such a tendency, the tabernacle was set up in Shiloh to promote a

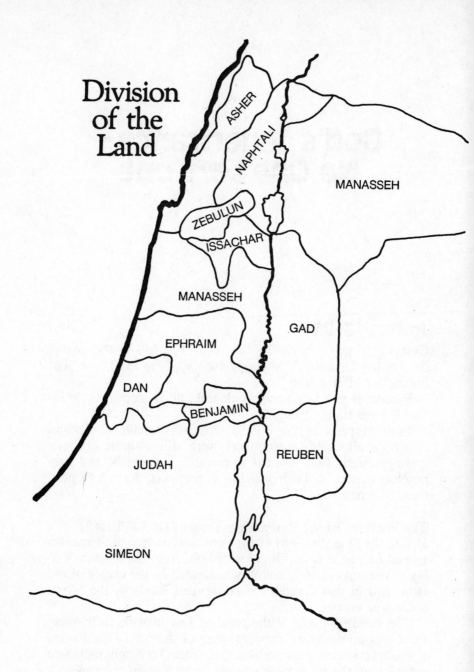

Division of the Land

ASHER

NAPHTALI

MANASSEH

ZEBULUN

ISSACHAR

MANASSEH

GAD

EPHRAIM

DAN

BENJAMIN

REUBEN

JUDAH

SIMEON

sense of national unity. It also served as a reminder to the people that the key to prosperity and blessing in the land was worship of Jehovah.

Indeed worship is what held life together for the people and the nation. A Puritan testified, "Wherever I have a house, there God shall have an altar." But the concept of the centrality of God in human life has fallen on hard times. Professor Arthur Holmes observed,

The bits and pieces of a man's life pull him in a hundred directions, unless he has within himself something to hold them together. But our day has no integrating world-view. There was a time when the religious outlook unified life in Western society. Think of the British or European countryside: the first sign of an approaching town is the church spire that soars above everything else and around which, it seems, the whole community once clustered. In place of this we now have the high-rise, the factory belt, or the corn silo, symbols of our materialism, or the sprawling metropolis that has no unifying theme unless it be the decentralized existence of fragmented man (*The Idea of a Christian College,* Eerdmans, p. 115).

When the Israelites assembled for the celebration of the new worship center, Joshua sensed that a feeling of war-weariness had overtaken them. They were exhausted in the struggle for the conquest of Canaan; and yet Joshua sharply reproached them. "How long will you put off entering to take possession of the land which the Lord, the God of your fathers, has given you?" (18:33) It was apparently the responsibility of the tribes to initiate matters relating to allocation of territory. Every passing day was a day lost in the program of completely occupying the land, and a day in which the enemy could return or become more firmly entrenched.

Joshua was for action, but not before careful preparations were made. Appointing a commission of 21 men, 3 from each of 7 tribes, he sent them to make a topographical survey of the remaining land. This complex task required time and skill. Josephus declares that these men were experts in geometry, and it is probable that they mastered the science of land surveying, as young men in Egypt. Who among them dreamed they would ever put that knowledge to use so strategically in their land of promise? God has a way of using our background and experiences if we offer them all to Him.

After writing their expert observations in a book, the surveyors returned to Shiloh where Joshua proceeded to cast lots to determine the portions of territory to be allotted to the remaining seven tribes.

1. The territory of Benjamin (18:11-28). By the hand of God, Benjamin was assigned the land that lay between Judah and Ephraim, thus minimizing the incipient rivalry between these two leading tribes. While the area was covered by mountains and ravines, extending only 25 miles from east to west, and 15 miles at its widest point from north to south, it included many cities important to biblical history—Jericho, Bethel, Gibeon, Ramah, Mizpeh, and Jerusalem. Thus the ultimate site of the temple was in Benjamin, fulfilling Moses' prophecy (Deut. 33:12).

2. The territory of Simeon (19:1-9). In fulfillment of Jacob's prophecy (Gen. 49:5-7), and because Judah could not cope with the large area assigned to her, Simeon was given land in the southern section of Judah's territory. But it was not long before Simeon lost individuality as a tribe, for her territory was eventually incorporated into Judah, and many of her citizens migrated north to Ephraim and Manasseh (2 Chron. 15:9; 34:6). This explains how after the division of the kingdom following Solomon, there were ten tribes in the north and but two—Judah and Benjamin—in the south.

3. The territory of Zebulun (19:10-16). According to Jacob's prophecy, Zebulun would "dwell at the seashore; and . . . be a haven for ships" (Gen. 49:13). She was assigned a portion in lower Galilee, which many consider to have been landlocked; however, a strip of land extended to the Mediterranean Sea forming an enclave in Issachar's territory. The city of Nazareth was within the borders of Zebulun's allotment.

4. *The territory of Issachar (19:17-23).* Lying east of Zebulun and south of the Sea of Galilee, Issachar was to occupy the fertile and beautiful valley of Jezreel, also a noted battlefield. Until the time of David, however, the people remained in the mountainous district on the eastern end of the valley.

5. *The territory of Asher (19:24-31).* Asher was assigned the Mediterranean coastal lands from Mt. Carmel north to Tyre and Sidon. By virtue of her vital position, she was to protect Israel from northern coastal enemies such as the Phoenicians. By David's time Asher had faded into insignificance, though her tribal identity was not lost. Anna the prophetess, who along with Simeon gave thanks for the birth of Jesus, was from the tribe of Asher (Luke 2:36-38).

6. *The territory of Naphtali (19:32-39).* Adjacent to Asher on the east, Naphtali had the Jordan River and Sea of Galilee as its eastern boundary. While not highly significant in the Old Testament period, Naphtali occupied lands that were important in New Testament history because the Galilean ministry of Jesus Christ was centered there. The Prophet Isaiah contrasted the early gloom, due to Assyrian invasion, and later glory of this district:

But there will be no more gloom for her who was in anguish; in earlier times He treated the land of Zebulun and the land of Naphtali with contempt, but later on He shall make it glorious, by the way of the sea, on the other side of Jordan, Galilee of the Gentiles. The people who walk in darkness will see a great light; those who live in a dark land, the light will shine on them (Isa. 9:1-2).

7. *The territory of Dan (19:40-48).* It appears that the least desirable portion fell to Dan. Surrounded by Ephraim

and Benjamin on the north and east, and by Judah on the south, Dan's boundaries coincided with theirs. Only cities are included. Not only was the original location too small, but when part of the territory of Dan was lost to the Amorites (Jud. 1:34), the majority of the tribe migrated to the far north, settling in Leshem (Laish) opposite the northern sector of Naphtali.

Thus God provided for the needs of each tribe. Though in some cases a part of the inheritance was still in the hands of the enemy, the Israelites were to possess it by faith, trusting God to enable them to defeat their foes. Failing to do so would mean poverty and weakness, conditions God did not plan for His people.

A number of years ago newspapers carried the story of a search on Chicago's skid row for a British man who was the sole heir to $12 million. The poor man's situation was tragic —he had access to great wealth but was living in abject poverty. Israel faced that danger, and so do we unless we appropriate by faith the spiritual blessings God intends us to have as Christians.

The Special Provision for Joshua (19:49-51)

Whereas Caleb's inheritance was determined first, Joshua's was last! Only after all of the tribes had received their allotments did Joshua ask for his. What a selfless spirit he possessed! And what a contrast his behavior provides to many of the leaders in our own time, who use their position and influence for self-enrichment.

Joshua's choice of land further revealed his humility. He asked for Timnath-serah, a city in the rugged, infertile, mountainous district of his own tribe. He could have appropriated land in the fairest and most productive area of Canaan. With deep appreciation for his godly leadership, the sons of Israel granted Joshua his modest request, and "he built the city [added to it] and settled in it" (v. 50b).

Thus in one of the final pictures of this stalwart leader, we see that Joshua was not only a fighter but also a builder. The combination is a rare one among God's servants.

The late Rev. William McCarrell, for many years the dedicated pastor of the Cicero Bible Church, Cicero, Illinois, was also a fighter. On one occasion, he confronted the faculty of a nearby university, challenging them face to face regarding their unscriptural teachings. He said he felt like Daniel in the lions' den. Another time he returned from lunch to discover that one of Al Capone's henchmen had delivered a cash contribution to the church office. With money in hand, McCarrell strode the few blocks to Capone's headquarters and tossed the contribution on the desk, explaining that he could not under any circumstances accept their donation.

But he was also a builder. Beginning with a small, struggling congregation, he built a dynamic and flourishing church. Yet that was not enough. Reaching out to other communities, he established more than 20 other Bible teaching churches, several of which have grown to significant size. He was a modern-day Joshua.

The Assignment of Cities of Refuge (20:1-9)
The law given to Moses provided for the future establishment of cities of refuge (Ex. 21:13). These cities, providing a haven for the unintentional manslayer, are dealt with in detail in Numbers 35 and Deuteronomy 19.

The fact that these cities are discussed in four books of the Old Testament suggests that the subject is of great importance. God wished to impress upon Israel the sanctity of human life. To take another person's life, even if unintentionally, is a very serious thing.

In the ancient world, blood revenge was widely practiced. When a person was killed, his nearest relative took responsibility for vengeance. The vendetta was often handed down from one generation to another, so that larger and larger numbers of innocent people died violently. Blaikie tells of a section of Italy in which, over a period of four centuries, more than

600,000 people were wounded or murdered out of revenge (*The Book of Joshua*, Hodder & Stoughton, p. 332). It is not hard to see the necessity for the cities of refuge.

A clear distinction is made in the Old Testament between premeditated murder and accidental manslaughter (Num. 35:11-16). In the case of murder, the nearest kinsman became the avenger of blood, to kill the guilty party. If a man killed another accidentally, he was provided a place of asylum in one of six cities of refuge (20:3). But he was to hurry to the nearest shelter without delay. According to Jewish tradition, the roads leading to the cities were kept in excellent condition and the crossroads were well marked with signposts reading, "Refuge! Refuge!" Runners were also stationed along the way to guide the fugitive.

Having arrived at the gate, the manslayer was to present his case (breathlessly!) to the elders of the city who formed an ancient court of law. (See Deut. 21:19; 22:15.) A provisional decision would then be made to grant him asylum until such time as a trial could be held, preferably before representatives of the community nearest the scene of the killing. If acquitted of premeditated murder, he was returned to the city of refuge where he lived until the death of the high priest, after which he was free to return to his home. Many have puzzled over the meaning of the death of the high priest in relation to the change in the status of the manslayer. It seems best to view it simply as a change in priestly administration which served as a statute of limitations ending the fugitive's exile in the city of refuge.

The six designated cities were located on both sides of the Jordan River. On the west side were Kadesh in Galilee, Shechem in Ephraim, and Hebron in Judah. The cities on the east side were Bezer in the south, Ramoth in the region of Gilead, and Golan in the northern territory of Bashan.

But we do not read in the Old Testament of a single instance in which this merciful provision of deliverance was utilized. Some critics suggest that the silence of Scripture indicates these cities were not part of the Mosaic legislation but a provision instituted after the exile. Yet the post-exilic books likewise contain no reference to their use, and so it is further suggested by other critics that they were not occupied until the time of Christ.

In the face of such shifting arguments, it is much better to recognize the historicity of these accounts and explain the silence of the record by the obvious fact that the scriptural authors were selective about what they recorded. It was more important that the provision be made, than to document specific cases of use.

Some Christians claim that the provision of the cities of refuge is typical of the believer's salvation in Christ. Their benefit of sanctuary does remind us of Psalm 46:1: "God is our Refuge and Strength, a very present help in trouble"; and of Romans 8:1: "There is therefore now no condemnation for those who are in Christ Jesus."

The writer of the Epistle to the Hebrews must have had the Old Testament cities of refuge in mind when he wrote that believers have strong encouragement, having "fled for refuge in laying hold of the hope set before us" (Heb. 6:18b). We may properly conclude then that the cities of refuge are typical of Christ to whom the sinner may flee for refuge pursued by the avenging law which decrees judgment and death. In fact the great and key expression of the epistles, "in Christ," may also be connected here in an antitypical sense. For in Christ there is safety and security for every believer.

One of the most impressive art masterpieces in the world is Michelangelo's painting of the Last Judgment, on the ceiling of the Sistine Chapel in Rome. The focus of attraction is Jesus Christ the implacable Judge; and viewers are struck with awe and feelings of deep emotion, as they consider the inevitable final day of reckoning. Michelangelo himself was filled with anxiety and fear as he worked on this painting, realizing his own unworthiness to stand before God. But no person need be frightened by thoughts of judgment. Instead, for those who flee to Christ for refuge there is forgiveness, peace, hope, and eternal life.

The Appointment of Levitical Cities (21:1-45)

In the last and crowning act of distribution, the leaders of the tribe of Levi stepped forward to claim the cities which had been promised to them by Moses (Num. 35:1-8). These 48 cities with pastureland, including the 6 cities of refuge, were now assigned to the Levites. The three main branches of the tribe of Levi were named for Levi's three sons—Kohath, Gershon, and Merari.

The Kohathites had 23 cities, 13 in the tribes of Judah, Benjamin, and Simeon for the priests, the descendants of Aaron, and 10 more cities in Ephraim, Dan, and western Manasseh for the other branches of the Kohathites. Thus the priestly cities fell ultimately within the southern kingdom of Judah where the temple would be built in its capital city, Jerusalem.

The Gershonite cities were located in eastern Manasseh, Issachar, Asher, and Naphtali.

Merari received cities in Zebulun and in the Transjordanian tribes of Reuben and Gad.

This scattering of the tribe of Levi among the other tribes marked the fulfillment of Jacob's curse on Levi, along with Simeon, for their senseless murder of the Shechemites (Gen. 49:5, 7). In the case of Levi's descendants, God overruled to preserve their tribal identity and make them a blessing to all Israel. He did this because the Levites stood with Moses at a time of acute crisis (Ex. 32:26) and because Phinehas, a Levite, vindicated God's righteous name in the plains of Moab (Num. 25).

But at the time of the assignment, many of the cities were under Canaanite control and had to be conquered. The Levites did not always succeed in battle, and the other tribes did not offer to help. This would appear to be the simplest explanation for the lack of complete correlation between the list of levitical cities here and in 1 Chronicles 6:54-81.

The potential for good in the dispersion of Levites among the other tribes, was almost unlimited. Moses, in his final blessing of the tribes, said of the Levites, "They shall teach Thine ordinances to Jacob, and Thy law to Israel" (Deut. 33:10). The solemn responsibility and high privilege of the Levites was to instruct Israel in the law of the Lord and to maintain the knowledge of His Word among the people. Especially in the north and east, the Levites ought to have been barriers against the idolatry of Tyre and Sidon, and the heathen practices of the desert tribes and Damascus.

It has been estimated that no one in Israel lived more than 10 miles from a city in which Levites had their residence. Thus every Israelite was close to a man well-versed in the Law of Moses, someone who could give advice and counsel on the many problems of religious, family, or political life. It was so essential that Israel obey the Word of God in all areas of life; without this their prosperity would cease and their privileges would be forfeited.

The Levites did not live up to their potential or fulfill their mission. Declared Blaikie, "If the Levites had all been consecrated men, idolatry and its great brood of corruptions would never have spread over the land of Israel" (*The Book of Joshua*, p. 352).

Perhaps too many of the Levites succumbed, as many of us do, to the softening influences of the "good life." When Eddie Arcaro retired as one of the nation's most successful racing jockies back in 1962, a reporter asked him if he still got up early to walk his mounts around the track while the dew was still on the ground. Arcaro confessed frankly, "It becomes difficult to get up early once a guy starts wearing silk pajamas."

All the territory had been allocated. God had kept His promise to give Israel the land, rest on every side, and victory over their enemies.

The Lord faithfully performed every part of His obligation.

This is not to affirm that at any given point, every corner of the land was in Israel's possession; for God Himself had told Israel they would conquer the land gradually (Deut. 7:22). Nor can we ignore the tragedies that developed in the period of the Judges, and which were Israel's fault.

Yet the unfaithfulness of Israel in no way impugns the faithfulness of God. Paul reminds us of this fact in his words to Timothy, "If we are faithless, He remains faithful; for He cannot deny Himself" (2 Tim. 2:13).

Israel now occupied the land as God had promised. God does keep His word. He can be counted on to fulfill what He promises. He does not walk out on His commitments.

"The promises of God, in Him they are yes" (2 Cor. 1:20).

11
The Danger
of Misjudging Motives

Joshua 22

In the beautiful lake country of England, the haunt of many English poets, there is a peak of land over a lakeshore called Point Rash Judgment. On one occasion Wordsworth, his sister, and Coleridge were walking along the shore when they saw a man fishing in a distant boat. Since it was the harvest season when all ablebodied men were working in the fields, the poets were harshly critical of the fisherman until on closer sight they saw he was aged and weak. Struck with the falsity and unkindness of their criticism, they named the place "Point Rash Judgment."

Israel made a similar mistake. A rash and impetuous judgment, made when the eastern tribes returned to their own inheritance, threatened the newly settled communities with civil war. It was a dangerous and potentially explosive situation. But in the providence of God the tragedy was averted and Israel learned some valuable and important lessons.

The Admonition of Joshua (22:1-8)

The eastern tribes of Reuben, Gad, and the half-tribe of Manasseh had performed well. They were called before Joshua who commended them for keeping their word to God, and for fighting alongside their brothers in all of the struggles of the conquest of Canaan. For seven long years these men had been separated from their wives and families. Now the battles were over, the land was divided, and it was time to go home.

Joshua dismissed the 40,000 soldiers with honor. Re-creating the scene Francis Schaeffer states,

> If we use a little imagination, we can feel the tremendous emotion involved in the parting of these comrades-at-arms. We can picture the men going through the camp, finding the friends with whom they had fought side by side and saying good-bye to some who had even saved their lives. They shook hands and they parted, as worshipers of God, as friends and fellow companions in war. There is a comradeship among men in titanic moments that is one of the great "mystiques" of life. It is the explanation of the mystique of the rope—two men on a mountain battling nature together, depending for their very lives on a common rope (*Joshua and the Flow of Biblical History,* InterVarsity Press, p. 174).

As the weary but happy soldiers left, they took with them a substantial share of the spoil taken from the enemy. Joshua had instructed them to share the booty with their brothers who had remained at home. But why should those who had not endured any of the pain and peril of the conflict enjoy any of the spoil?

Some of those who remained behind would no doubt much rather have gone to war, but who then would have raised the crops and protected the women and children? The principle is firmly established that honors and rewards are not to go alone to those who carry arms, but also to those who stay home to perform the commonplace duties.

A Christian businessman recounted a conversation his father had many years ago with a Pullman porter.

> Dad was returning from six weeks of buying wool in Texas. From St. Louis he took the *Wolverine* to Boston. He had established a good relationship with the porter,

and they had several talks together about their mutual faith. The train was pulling out from Back Bay Station, and in a few minutes the trip would be over, and Dad would be at the South Station and a block from his Summer Street office. He was, naturally, excited about getting home and was ready to leave the train, when the porter approached him and said, "Mr. Emery, do you suppose I could ask you a question after my passengers leave?" So Dad remained and after the last passenger disembarked, the porter returned with his question.

"There were two boys in my family. My mother worked very hard to teach us all she could and to see that we had the best education available at that time. I was a good student. When I had graduated from high school, I went to work as a railroad waiter and then I got this job. My whole desire was to help my mother and fulfill her wish that I go to college and become a preacher. She wanted her life to count by seeing her son a preacher. Well, I saved my money and while I was doing this, my younger brother went in a different direction. He drank and partied and nearly killed himself by living for the devil. About the time I was accepted for college, my brother was converted. He decided he wanted to preach. He had nothing, so he asked me to provide for his education. I was so happy to see this great change in his life that I agreed, and today my brother is a nationally known preacher. You may have heard him on the radio. He has led thousands to Christ. So, you see, I couldn't go into the ministry and I am too old now. Mr. Emery, my question is this: Do you suppose the Lord will give me some credit for the souls my brother led to him?"

That night, at the dinner table, when my father told this story he was so deeply moved he nearly broke down. We knew what his answer would have been and that the biblical principle is expressed in 1 Samuel 30:24, "For as his share is who goes down to the battle, so shall his share be who stays by the baggage; they shall share alike" (RSV)" (Allan C. Emery, *A Turtle on a Fencepost:* Word Books, pp. 46-47).

The returning soldiers also left with the six solemn exhortations of Joshua ringing in their ears: "But take diligent heed to do the command and the Law . . . to love the Lord your God . . . to walk in all His ways . . . to keep His commandments . . . to cleave unto Him . . . to serve Him with all your heart and all your soul." The charge was short but passionate. Their military obligations were fulfilled, and Joshua was reminding them of their abiding spiritual commitments which were conditions for the continued blessing of God. Like an anxious parent who sees a son or daughter leave home for a place where they could be separated from spiritual influences, so Joshua delivered his earnest charge to the departing warriors. He was fearful that their separation from the rest of the tribes might cause them to drift away from the worship of Jehovah and to embrace idolatry.

The Symbolic Action of the Eastern Tribes (22:9-11)
Leaving Shiloh, the armies of the eastern tribes headed excitedly for home. As they approached the Jordan River, their minds were probably filled with memories of the miraculous crossing seven years before, of the remarkable victory over nearby Jericho, and of the other triumphs shared with their brothers from whom they had so recently separated.

A sense of isolation from the other tribes began to sweep over them. But this was not simply because an ordinary river would separate the eastern from the western tribes, for the Jordan is not an ordinary river. Mountains on each side rise to heights above 2,000 feet and the Jordan valley nestled in between is in effect a great trench 5 to 13 miles wide. During a part of the year the intense heat greatly discourages travelers. This then was a very pronounced river boundary and contributed to the fear of these tribesmen that they and their brethren would permanently drift apart. After all, out of sight is often out of mind.

What then could be done to keep alive the ties of comradeship forged by those long years of united struggles? What could be done to symbolize the unity between the people on both sides of the river, to remind everyone that they were all the children of the promise? The answer that suggested itself to the minds of these soldiers was that they should build a huge altar, one that could be seen from a great distance, and which would witness to their right to the original altar at the tabernacle.

So such an altar was erected on the western side of the Jordan River. Why did they not build some other kind of monument? Because they knew that the true basis of their unity was their common worship centered in the sacrifices at the altar.

The Threat of War (22:12-20)

However, this symbol of unity was misconstrued to be a symbol of apostasy! When word reached the other tribes, they gathered at Shiloh, the site of the one true altar, and prepared to go to war against the armies of the eastern tribes. On the basis of what they had heard, the Israelites concluded that this was rebellion against God. They thought that the others had set up a second altar of sacrifice contrary to the Mosaic Law (Lev. 17:8-9).

They thought the holiness of God was being threatened. So these men, who were sick of war, said, "The holiness of God demands no compromise." I would to God that the church of the twentieth century would learn this lesson. The holiness of the God who exists demands that there be no compromise in the area of truth (Schaeffer, *Joshua and the Flow*, p. 175).

Is there compromise today in the area of truth? The late Professor Addison Leitch told of two seminary students who were instructed in certain classes not to use the Bible as a support for the positions they took. When one student argued from Scripture, he was laughed to scorn. Recent published reports tell of an ordained minister and a professor of religion who openly deny the unique deity of Jesus Christ and yet continue to serve in their positions.

Faced with apparent compromise and disobedience of God's commands, the Israelites called for a war of judgment against their brothers. And though we must admire their zeal for truth, their jealousy for purity of worship, we are relieved that wisdom prevailed over rashness. They decided to begin by vigorously remonstrating with the two and one-half tribes, in the hope that they would abandon their project. War could thereby be avoided.

It is dangerous to yield to suspicion without proof. It is wrong to judge people's motives simply on the basis of circumstantial evidence.

When Charles Haddon Spurgeon was a boy, he asked his mother for some eggs from her chickens. She answered, "You may have them if you pay for them." Rumors were circulated later that the Spurgeons were mean and grasping because they sold eggs, milk, and butter within the family. The Spurgeons gave no explanation and the critics continued to repeat their malicious gossip. At Mrs. Spurgeon's death, the explanation came out, when books recording profits from all sales were found with the note that all these profits were devoted to the support of two elderly widows of Welsh ministers.

Phinehas, noted for his righteous zeal for the Lord (Num. 25:6-18), headed a deputation of 10 tribal rulers whose responsibility was to confront the others. Arriving at the scene of the new altar, the appointed group charged the eastern tribesmen with unheard of wickedness, characterizing their action as a trespass, iniquity, and rebellion. They reminded them that the iniquity of Peor brought God's judgment on the whole nation (Num. 25), as did also the sin of Achan (Josh. 7). Now the entire congregation was in jeopardy once again because of their daring act of rebellion.

Then it was magnanimously suggested that if they felt the land east of Jordan was unclean—not hallowed by God's presence—the western tribes would make room for them on their side of the Jordan. This was a generous, loving offer, involving material cost.

Observes Schaeffer,

Once more, here is the tragedy of the modern church! Our spirituality and our brotherhood often stop at the point of material possessions. In the early church this was not so. The Christians had things in common not because there was a law to this effect, not because this was an enforced Marx-Engels communism, but because they loved each other. And a love that does not go down into the practical stuff of life, including money and possessions, is absolute junk! To think that love is talking softly rather than saying something sharply and that it is not carried down into the practical stuff of life is not biblical. We must say with tears that the orthodox evangelical church in our generation has been poor at this point (*Joshua and the Flow*, p. 177).

The Defense of the Eastern Tribes (22:21-29)

The Israelite delegation was now to learn how wrong their rash judgments and stern denunciations had been. The facts behind the construction of the altar by the Jordan now came to light.

Instead of responding to the fierce reproof in anger, the eastern tribes in candor and sincerity solemnly repudiated the charge that they in fact erected a rival altar in rebellion against God. Invoking God as a witness they swore twice by His three names—El, Elohim, Jehovah (the Mighty One, God, the Lord)—affirming that if their act was in rebellion against God and His commands concerning worship they deserved His judgment.

Why then was the second altar built? They explained earnestly that it was occasioned by the geographic separation of their people and the effect this might have on future generations.

> In time to come your sons may say to our sons, "What have you to do with the Lord, the God of Israel? For the LORD has made the Jordan a border between us and you, you sons of Reuben and sons of Gad; you have no portion in the LORD." So your sons may make our sons stop fearing the LORD (vv. 24-25).

The eastern tribesmen made it clear that they were fully aware of God's laws governing Israel's worship; their recently erected altar was not intended as a place for sacrifices and offerings, but as a witness to all generations that the Transjordanian tribes had a right to cross the Jordan and worship at Shiloh. This altar was only a copy of the true worship center and an evidence of their right to frequent that one.

While we must deeply admire their concern for the spiritual welfare of future generations it would appear that the action of the two and one-half tribes was unnecessary. God had ordained in the Law that all Israelite males were to appear at the sanctuary three times a year (Ex. 23:17). This, if heeded, would have preserved the unity of the tribes, both spiritually and politically.

The building of another altar was also a dangerous precedent. John J. Davis comments,

> The unifying factor in ancient Israel was not her culture, architecture, economy, or even military objectives. The long-range unifying factor was her worship of Jehovah. When the central sanctuary was abandoned as the true place of worship, the tribes then developed independent sanctuaries, thus alienating themselves from other tribes and weakening their military potential. The effects of this trend are fully seen in the period of the Judges (*Conquest and Crisis*, Baker, p. 87).

The Reconciliation of the Tribes (22:30-34)
There was a happy ending to this grave crisis as the explanation of the eastern tribes was fully accepted by Phinehas and

his delegation, as well as by the other tribes. In concluding the whole matter, Phinehas expressed deep gratitude that no sin had been committed and that the wrath of God therefore was not incurred.

In a book describing the occupation and distribution of the Promised Land, why should this single incident be treated in such detail? Simply because it illustrates certain principles that were vital to Israel living together in the land harmoniously and under God's full blessing. The same principles apply to those in God's family today.

• It is commendable for believers to be zealous for the purity of the faith. Compromise of truth is always costly. (See Jude 3.)

• It is wrong to judge people's motives on the basis of circumstantial evidence. We need to gather all the facts and to avoid a quick response on the basis of an emotionally charged account of a situation.

• Frank and open discussion will often clear the air and lead to reconciliation. But we must approach such a confrontation in a spirit of meekness, not arrogance. (See Gal. 6:1.)

• If we are wrongly accused, we would do well to remember the wise counsel of Solomon, "A gentle answer turns away wrath, but a harsh word stirs up anger" (Prov. 15:1).

12
The Sage Counsel
of an Old Soldier

Joshua 23-24

General Douglas MacArthur appeared before Congress on April 19, 1951 after being relieved of duties by President Truman. His address ended with these moving words:

The world has turned over many times since I took the oath on the plain at West Point, and the hopes and dreams have long since vanished: but I still remember the refrain of one of the most popular barracks ballads of that day which proclaimed most proudly that old soldiers never die; they just fade away. And like the old soldier in that ballad, I now close my military career and just fade away, an old soldier who tried to do his duty as God gave him the sight to see that duty.

So does the Book of Joshua end—with an old soldier saying farewell. His parting addresses are tinged with sadness, like all last words. And they express the deep concern of Joshua, for he observed a growing complacency on the part of Israel toward the remnants of the Canaanites, an easy acceptance of joint occupancy of a land which was to have been exclusively theirs.

With Israel's enemies practically vanquished, Joshua knew well the danger of his people letting down. Before his departure from active leadership, he felt compelled to warn them that continued obedience to God's commands was essential to continued enjoyment of His blessing.

Although some have suggested that in these final chapters we have two reports of the same event, it seems best to view chapter 23 as Joshua's challenge to Israel's leaders, and chapter 24 as his charge to the people.

Joshua's Final Challenge to the Leaders (23:1-16)

Some 15 or 20 years following the end of the conquest and distribution of the land, Joshua summoned Israel's leaders, probably to Shiloh where the tabernacle was located, to warn them earnestly of the dangers of departure from Jehovah. It was a solemn meeting—no doubt Caleb was there, Phinehas the priest, the soldiers of the conquest who had exchanged the sword for the plowshare and were now heads of families, elders, and judges.

They had come without hesitation to hear the last words of their great chief. And the old veteran wanted to speak on one theme—God's unfailing faithfulness to Israel and their corresponding responsibility to be faithful to Him. Three times he repeated his central message; three times he emphasized the faithfulness of God and the responsibility of Israel, fearful they would not hear and heed.

1. The first cycle (vv. 3-8). Avoiding any temptation to elevate himself, Joshua reminded the leaders of Israel that their enemies had been defeated solely because the Lord God had fought for them. The battles were not theirs but the Lord's. The psalmist reiterated this affirmation. "For by their own sword they did not possess the land; and their own arm did not save them; but Thy right hand, and Thine arm, and the light of Thy presence, for Thou didst favor them" (Ps. 44:3). As for the Canaanites who still lingered about the country, the Lord God would drive them out also so that Israel could inherit the land they occupied.

Turning to impress the Israelites with their responsibility,

Joshua passed on the very words Jehovah had armed him with as he was instructed to cross over the Jordan. Courage and obedience, the graces that led to the successful conquest of Canaan, were no less essential now. Specifically, Joshua dreaded Israel's conformity to the heathen nations around them and so forbade all contact and intimacy with them. He knew that the people would backslide step by step until, in the course of their decline, they would prostrate themselves before the shrines of the pagan deities.

Spiritual compromise is a gradual and insidious process. In the early church some Christians, to make a living, carved and gilded images for the pagans. Since they did not worship them nor bow in their shrines, they saw no harm in producing and polishing such images for sale. Their reasoning was, "After all, somebody will do it anyway—and I have to live." Replied Tertullian, the Christian apologist, "Must you live?"

Joshua and Tertullian joined in affirming that a believer has only one *must,* and that is to be faithful to the Lord.

2. The second cycle (vv. 9-13). Returning to his theme, Joshua again affirmed God's past faithfulness to Israel. Jehovah fought their battles for them, and while indeed some of the Canaanites remained in the land, wherever an enemy had been encountered he had been overcome.

Israel was then solemnly exhorted, on the basis of divine interventions on their behalf, to love God. This would require diligence and watchfulness because of the near presence of their corrupt neighbors. The temptation would be strong to forsake Jehovah and cleave to the people of Canaan; but this would be a fateful choice and one fraught with peril to Israel. This danger is graphically described by Joshua in terms of the dire results that would follow:

• God would no longer drive out these heathen people, but they would remain to mar Israel's inheritance.

• These Canaanites among them would be as snares and traps to entangle them, as scourges to lash them, and as thorns that fly back into the face stabbing the eyes.

• Miseries and troubles would increase for Israel until they would be dispossessed of their land.

Joshua did not contemplate any possibility of neutrality as he posed the choice to be made. It was either Israel's God or the men and values of Canaan. So it is today. There is no middle course. "No one can serve two masters" (Matt. 6:24).

In one of his fables, Aesop told of the time when the beasts and birds were engaged in war. The bat tried to belong to both parties. When the birds were victorious, he would fly around announcing that he was a bird; but when the beasts won a fight, he would assure everyone he was a beast. Soon his hypocrisy was discovered and he was rejected by both the beasts and the birds. As a result the bat can appear openly only at night.

Israel would one day pay a bitter price for failing to heed Joshua's warning, for trying to serve two masters. "Like the spotted leopard, with its graceful form and gentle gait, so is the faltering, fawning world. Who would suspect danger? But cleave thereunto, and ere long its strength and cruelty will appear, and its miserable victims will be torn to pieces in its teeth and talons" (G.W. Butler, *The Lord's Host,* William Oliphant, p. 322).

3. The third cycle (vv. 14-16). Like a masterful preacher, Joshua recapitulated his discourse, this time as a dying man, hoping his words would sink more deeply into their hearts. Once more he spoke of God's punctilious faithfulness to every promise; once more he warned of the doom of the disobedient.

Joshua's deep anxiety concerned the nations that were left; as the old soldier looked into the future, he foresaw Israel's sinful compromise with them and the tragic fate that would inevitably overtake the people of God.

The terrible climax of this message to the nation's leaders emphasized the fact that Israel's greatest danger was not military. It was moral and spiritual. And if Joshua were alive today, the strong likelihood is that he would say the same thing to us. Military strategists and politicians agree that we are in grave danger. Few, however, are discussing our moral and spiritual problems as a nation.

In 1954 Dr. Gerhard Schroeder, then West German Federal Minister of the Interior, made this prophetic utterance:

It was the stimulating conviction of our grandfathers that civilization on the basis of *technical progress was bound to lead to permanent improvement* of the world and *finally to a happy solution of all its problems.*

A few thinkers tried to criticize this optimism as naive. Today they seem to us great prophets who anticipated the present crisis.

More and more, philosophers, historians, and poets of the different nations have pointed out that *belief in the progress of the world is an error.*

The political events, the social revolutions, and the confusion of philosophical thought at the present time have *confirmed these pessimistic prophecies.*

The optimism of the past has turned into *dark pessimism!*

Comments Richard Halverson,

More than two decades have passed since that statement was made in 1954 and the *cumulative experience* has served to confirm the "dark pessimism."

Not only are we not solving our human problems— *they are compounding* . . . crime, drug abuse, alcoholism, divorce, terrorism, child abuse, wife abuse, etc.

We have become *technological giants* . . . and *moral adolescents.*

Our progress in ethics and morals and humanness has declined in *inverse ratio* to our technical and scientific expertise.

Man is *truly human only as he is rightly related to God.* Sin is man's self-alienation from God.

Jesus Christ came into history to restore man's *relationship with God.* "Be reconciled to God" (2 Cor. 5:20) (*Perspective*, April 8, 1980).

Joshua's Final Charge to the People (24:1-28)

Joshua's last meeting with the people took place at Shechem. Whether this second gathering occurred soon after the previous one, whether it was held on an anniversary of the earlier, or whether it was after a long interval, cannot be determined.

The geographical setting is of interest. Shechem, a few miles northwest of Shiloh, was the place where Abraham first received the promise that God would give his seed the land of Canaan. Abraham responded by building an altar to demonstrate his faith in the one true God (Gen. 12:6-7).

Jacob too stopped at Shechem on his return from Padan-aram and buried there the idols his family had brought with them (Gen. 35:4). When the Israelites completed the first phase of the conquest of Canaan, they journeyed to Shechem where Joshua built an altar to Jehovah, inscribed the Law of God on stone pillars, and reviewed these laws for all the people (Josh. 8:30-35).

There was good reason therefore for Joshua to convene the Israelites at this location. Certainly the stones on which the Law had been written were still standing, vivid reminders of that whole significant event. But from this moment on, the beautiful valley between Mt. Ebal and Mt. Gerizim would be associated with this poignant farewell scene, as their honored leader spoke to them for the last time, perhaps with an old and quavering voice.

The literary form of this discourse has occasioned a great deal of interest and comment as well. It is now rather well-known that the rulers of the Hittite Empire in this period (1450-1200 B.C.) established international agreements with their vassal states, obligating them to serve the king in faithfulness and obedience. These suzerainty treaties followed a regular pattern and required periodic renewal.

It seems quite clear that in Joshua 24 we have, in the standard suzerainty treaty form of this time, a covenant renewal document in which the people of Israel were called upon to confirm their convenant relationship with their God.

The Mosaic Covenant established at Sinai was not an everlasting covenant; hence it had to be renewed in every generation. That renewal was now transacted in a formal and impressive ceremony.

1. Reviewing their blessings (vv. 1-13). The opening two verses identify the Lord God as Author of the Covenant and Israel as the vassal people. Following this preamble is the historical prologue, reviewing God's past blessing upon His subjects. He brought them out of Ur of the Chaldees, out of Egypt, and into Canaan.

It was God who spoke in this recapitulation of Israel's history. No less than 17 times the personal pronoun "I" was used—"I took. . . . I gave. . . . I sent. . . . I plagued. . . . I brought. . . . I delivered." Any greatness Israel achieved was not by their effort but through God's grace and enablement. From first to last Israel's conquests, deliverances, and prosperity were of the good mercies of God and not of their own making.

Is this not what every believer is forced to acknowledge? What we are and have by God's grace we owe to Him.

John Newton, the slave trader who became a Christian, wrote a text in large letters, and hung it above his mantelpiece: "Thou shalt remember that thou wast a bondman in the land of Egypt, and the Lord thy God redeemed thee" (Deut. 15:15, KJV).

Whether studying the Old Testament or the New, we are reminded that we are not where we are because of a long, wise, and godly heritage. We come from rebellion. Individually, we are children of wrath. After we are Christians, we must look at others who are still under God's wrath and always say, "I am essentially what you are. If I am in a different place, it is not because I am intrinsically better than you, but simply because God has done something in my life." There is no place for pride (Francis Schaeffer, *Joshua and the Flow of Biblical History*, InterVarsity Press, p. 206).

2. Rehearsing their responsibilities (vv. 14-24). The stipulations of the covenant renewal were then stated: Israel must fear Jehovah and serve Him. In the Hittite treaties, foreign alliances were prohibited; so in this covenant Israel was to reject alliances with all foreign gods. Joshua boldly challenged them to choose between the gods of Ur their ancestors worshiped—the gods of Egypt, the gods of the Amorites—and Jehovah. Then, adding example to exhortation, Israel's venerated leader assured them that whatever their choice, *his* mind was made up, *his* course clear: "As for me and my house, we will serve the LORD" (v. 15).

The people responded with alacrity, moved by the force of Joshua's arguments and the magnetism of his example. They despised the very thought of forsaking the God who had delivered them out of Egypt, protected them in the wilderness, and brought them into the land of promise. "Far be it from us that we should forsake the Lord to serve other gods" (v. 16).

Joshua spoke a second time. He was not at all satisfied with their burst of enthusiasm. Did he detect some traces of insincerity? Had he hoped that the people would bring forth their idols for destruction, as Jacob's family had done here some centuries before? There was no such response and Joshua bluntly declared, "Ye will not be able to serve the LORD, for He is a holy God. He is a jealous God; He will not forgive your transgression or your sins. If you forsake the LORD and serve foreign gods, then He will turn and do you harm and consume you after He has done good to you" (vv. 19-20).

Of course Joshua did not mean that God is not a God of forgiveness. He meant that God is not to be worshiped nor served lightly, and that to deliberately forsake Him to serve idols would be a presumptuous, willful, highhanded sin for which there is no forgiveness under the Law (Num. 15:30). The people once more responded to Joshua's probing words, earnestly reaffirming their purpose to serve Jehovah.

Joshua spoke a third time, pointedly challenging them to

serve as witnesses against themselves if they did turn aside from God. And the people immediately replied, "We are witnesses" (v. 22).

Joshua spoke a fourth and final time, coming to the point he had been building toward: "Now therefore, put away the foreign gods which are in your midst" (23a). He had heard the pledge on their lips; now he challenged them to prove their sincerity by their works. Knowing that many of them were secretly practicing idolatry, Joshua forthrightly demanded that they remove the foreign gods from their midst. Without the slightest hesitation the people shouted, "We will serve the LORD our God, and will obey His voice" (v. 24).

There could be no mixing of allegiance to God with idol worship. A firm choice had to be made then, as in every generation. Men must choose between expediency and principle, between this world and eternity, between God and idols.

What shape is an idol? I worship Ganesa, brother, god of worldly wisdom, patron of shopkeepers. He is in the shape of a little fat man with an elephant's head; he is made of soapstone and has two small rubies for eyes. What shape do you worship?

I worship a fishtail Cadillac convertible, brother. All my days I give it offerings of oil and polish. Hours of my time are devoted to its ritual; and it brings me luck in all my undertakings; and it establishes me among my fellows as a success in life. What model is your car, brother?

I worship my house beautiful, sister. Long and loving meditation have I spent on it; the chairs contrast with the rug, the curtains harmonize with the woodwork, all of it is perfect and holy. The ashtrays are in exactly the right places, and should some blasphemer drop ashes on the floor, I nearly die of shock. I live only for the service of my house, and it rewards me with the envy of my sisters, who must rise up and call me blessed. Lest my children profane the holiness of my house with dirt and noise, I drive them out-of-doors. What shape is your idol, sister?

Is it your house, or your clothes, or perhaps even your worthwhile and cultural club?

I worship the pictures I paint, brother. . . . I worship my job. . . . I worship my golf game. . . . I worship my comfort; after all, isn't enjoyment the goal of life? I worship my church; I want to tell you, the work we've done in missions beats all other denominations in this city, and next year we can afford that new organ, and you won't find a better choir anywhere. . .

What shape is your idol? (Joy Davidson, *Smoke on the Mountain,* The Westminster Press, pp. 30-31)

3. *The reminders of their pledge (vv. 25-28).* Realizing that further words would be fruitless, satisfied with the genuineness and sincerity of the people's consecration, Joshua solemnly renewed the covenant. He then proceeded to write down the agreement "in the Book of the Law of God" (v. 26a). This was no doubt deposited by the Ark of the Covenant (Deut. 31:24-27). Among the Hittites, likewise, the suzerainty treaty was placed in the sanctuary of the vassal state.

As a final reminder Joshua also apparently inscribed the statutes of the covenant on a large stone slab, which was set up beneath the oak belonging to this sacred location. Archeologists excavating the site of Shechem have uncovered a great limestone pillar which may be identified with the memorial referred to here. Joshua constituted the stone a witness, as if it had heard all of the transactions of the covenant.

Thus leading the people of Israel in a sacred ritual of covenant renewal by which they pledged to fear and follow the Lord God, Joshua completed his last public act. With the memories of this solemn occasion indelibly impressed on their minds, the Israelites returned to their homes in possession of their inheritance.

Three Peaceful Graves (24:29-33)

Three burials mark the close of the Book of Joshua. First it is recorded that Joshua died at an advanced age of 110 years and was buried in his own town. No greater tribute could be paid to this man than the fact that he was called simply "the servant of the Lord." He aspired to no greater rank than this. The sacred historian also took note of the high esteem in which Joshua was held at the time of his death, "And Israel served the LORD all the days of Joshua and all the days of the elders who survived Joshua."

What a contrast is seen in the words of a noted British historian who said recently of certain contemporary leaders, "They are men who cannot control their passions, keep their wives faithful to themselves or their sons out of brothels—and we look to them to control international tempers and preserve peace!"

The burial of Joseph's bones is also recorded. His dying request was that he be buried in the Promised Land. Now after the long years of the wanderings and the conquest, his remains were laid to rest in his father Jacob's field in Shechem.

The third burial was of the high priest Eleazar, son and successor of Aaron. It was his privilege to be associated with Joshua in the distribution of the land (Num. 34:17), and to direct the ministry of tabernacle worship in the crucial years of the conquest and settlement of Canaan.

Three burials—it seems a strange way to end the Book of Joshua! But these three peaceful graves testify to the faithfulness of God, for Joshua, Joseph, and Eleazar once lived in a foreign nation where they were the recipients of God's promise to take His people back to Canaan. Now all three were at rest *within* the borders of the Promised Land. God kept His Word to Joshua, Joseph, Eleazar—and to all Israel. And by this we are encouraged to count on the unfailing faithfulness of God.

Great is Thy faithfulness, O God my Father,
There is no shadow of turning with Thee;
Thou changest not, Thy compassions, they fail not;
As Thou hast been Thou forever wilt be.

Great is Thy faithfulness! Great is Thy faithfulness!
Morning by morning new mercies I see;
All I have needed Thy hand hath provided—
Great is Thy faithfulness, Lord, unto me!

William M. Runyon